Violent Sheep

The Tyranny of the Meek
Violent Sheep

Michelle Cole

NYT
Times
BOOKS

Acknowledgement is gratefully made to the following for their permission to reprint from copyright materials:

Herbert Gold for his article originally published as "The Post-Hip Generation of Frisco." Copyright © 1977 by Herbert Gold. Reprinted by permission.
Francis J. Moriarty for his article, "The New Men's Lib: Hands Off!" which originally appeared in the Los Angeles Times. Copyright © 1976.
Author-teacher Alan Cliburn for his article which originally appeared in the Los Angeles Herald Examiner. Copyright © 1978 by Alan Cliburn.
The Los Angeles Times for the article "Study Ignored in Approval of $2 Million Anticrime Proposal" by Robert Fairbanks. Copyright © 1978 by the Los Angeles Times. Reprinted by permission.
The New York Times for the article "Apolitical American Consultants" by Ann Crittendon. Copyright © 1975 by The New York Times Company. Reprinted by permission.
The Washington Post for the September 15, 1978 article "The Coming Information War" by John M. Eger. Copyright © 1978 by the Washington Post. Reprinted by permission.
New Directions Publishing Company for the exerpt from Who Are We Now by Lawerence Ferlinghetti. Copyright © 1976 by Lawerence Ferlinghetti. Reprinted by permission of New Directions.
Laff Records for the exerpt from their album "Craps After Hours" by Richard Pryor. Copyright © 1971 by Laff Records. By courtesy of Laff Records.

Published by TIMES BOOKS, a division of Quadrangle/The New York Times Book Co., Inc.
Three Park Avenue, New York, N.Y. 10016

Published simultaneously in Canada by Fitzhenry & Whiteside, Ltd., Toronto

Library of Congress Cataloging in Publication Data

Cole, Michelle, 1940–
    Violent sheep.

    1. Violence. 2. Passivity (Psychology)
3. Civilization, Modern—20th century. I. Title.
BF575.A3C55   1980   301.11   79–51426
ISBN 0–8129–0833–3

Manufactured in the United States of America

For Larry whose unending patience and support enabled me to make the invisible tangible

Acknowledgments

This book was deeply influenced by my association with Little Luis, Scarface, Harry, Nuny, Hector, Mike, Kiki, Rafael, Mousie, and Sampson who showed me what I didn't want to see. For that I am forever indebted to them.

I owe a special debt of gratitude to Stuart Black whose care and moral support helped me through many troubled times and led me to some inescapable conclusions about dependability.

My thanks also go to the late Margaret Mead who generously gave me sharp criticism and unquestioning support.

A special thanks goes to Joseph Rosner for the time he spent on the manuscript and for the humor and insights he shared with me, and to Steve Gelman for his unique understanding and talent.

Thanks also go to Bob Pickett.

Contents

Introduction   xi

I Our New Violence: A Redefinition   1

   Taking the Wool From Our Eyes   3
   Passive Violence   9
   Violent Passivity   19
   Biological Determinism   23

II Our New Aggressors: The Flock   29

   The Crisis Monger   33
   The Lummox   40
   The Conspicuous Non-assumer   44
   The Connection   50
   Babes   55
   The Systems Tangler   60
   The Victim   67
   The Innocent Bystander   72
   The Power Swindler   75
   The Web Spinner   79
   The Closet Competitor   85
   The Fortress   88
   The Blackmailer   94
   The Reluctant Champ   98
   The Gentle Provocateur   100

                                                       ix

III   Our New Society: Sheep Without Shepherds   103

    The Incredible Shrinking Man   105
    Leveling: Making the Piper Pay   109
    Idea Warping   119
    The Expertocracy: Little Lost Shepherds   132
    Rah Rah Blacksheep   158
    Green Pastures: Relearning Relationships   167

Introduction

The first time I saw a sixties love child hit a policeman with a flower, with the same contorted face that I had seen on policemen when they used their clubs on demonstrators, I knew that violence has a broader meaning than as it is generally defined.

Without seeing any physical destruction or struggle, without seeing any blood, I have since heard people talk about feeling crushed, beaten, wiped out, trampled, squeezed, defeated, and even dead. Victims of psychic violence, these people didn't know what hit them.

The purpose of this book is to define what hit them and to suggest how some forms of passive and psychic violence affect our daily lives.

I

Our New Violence
A Redefinition

Taking the Wool From our Eyes

It's not nice to be violent. We are taught very early to be nice. Consequently most people oppose violence except in self-defense or other extenuating circumstances. As extenuating circumstances increase and we feel a growing need to defend ourselves, we end up resorting to force. But this force is not always physical and often not easily identifiable. It's an undercover violence that enables us to defend ourselves and still see ourselves as nice. Although we've found new and intricate ways to practice this self-deception, we're not the first people to disguise reality through language and other tactics.

"He took the report," Leo Tolstoy wrote of Czar Nicholas I in "Hadji Murad," "and in his large handwriting wrote on its margin '. . . Deserves death, but, thank God, we have no capital punishment and it is not for me to introduce it. Make him run the gauntlet of a thousand men twelve times—Nicholas.' " In prescribing this punishment for a student who had attacked a professor, Tolstoy continued, "Nicholas knew that twelve thousand strokes with the regulation rods were not only certain death with torture, but were a superfluous cruelty . . . but it pleased him to be ruthlessly cruel and it also pleased him to think that we have abolished capital punishment in Russia."

On any given day in our society a person is almost certain to run gauntlets of less deadly but equally mendacious disguised violence.

I'm waiting in a supermarket express checkout line. The display copy of *The National Enquirer* is penetrating my subconscious with headlines about a food I eat every day which causes cancer in mice. It's been a long day, I'm frazzled, and the line isn't moving.

A man whose groceries have just been bagged is arguing with the checker. I can't hear what the issue is, but his revenge is to count his change two or three times, slowly, before digging through his bags for his register receipt. Then he very leisurely takes everything out of the bags and checks the items against the

3

receipt. The people in line are getting restless. Some "get on" the checker the way frustrated motorists blame the visible traffic cop who is trying to untangle a rush hour mess. A few of us yell to the man to move over. He responds by moving even more slowly. He's teaching us a lesson: The more we bitch the longer he's going to stand there.

Finally, when his unstated, non-physical attack has made its point and he has "won," he moves to leave, then stops, pulls out his money, and asks for a pack of cigarettes. Getting in that one last punch, he slowly counts his change again. Then he is gone, through the automatic doors to the parking lot.

Everyone is visibly relieved when the ten-minute incident ends and the line begins to move at a quick pace. Some people shake their heads and sigh, but there is nothing much to talk about. Though we have been briefly held hostage in an unreported kidnapping, it was just an everyday event. Despite the physical and emotional discomfort, nothing significant has happened. Nothing to go home and tell anyone about.

Most people experience these "non-events" frequently and dismiss them as irritating trivialities. Still, whenever I mention the latest violent non-event in my life, a flood of similar stories come from those around me. They tell stories that they had put into mental limbo, that have been waiting for a chance to come out.

I see less danger in experiencing these malignant events than in our inability to define or understand them. Denied, disguised, and diffused violence disorients people and makes a lot of them sick and crazy.

"I was paged and told to 'slip by the office,' " an executive of a Baltimore company reports. "My specific feeling of foreboding was reinforced by the diffuse sense of impending disaster that had pervaded the factory for some months.

"At the office my boss handed me a formal looking paper he said he had just received from the chain of command.

" 'As much a surprise to me as to you,' he added, thereby relieving himself of responsibility. No wonder. I was laid off . . . seemingly by invisible forces. . . ."

Tens of thousands of others have lost their jobs in equally antiseptic scenes. The entire language of firing an employee has changed to create a disarming and enormous gap between the action and the possibility of an appropriate reaction. Executives are no longer fired. They are "displaced," "separated," or "terminated." They are not incompetent, only "redundant." Corporations, understanding the violence they are perpetrating, try to diffuse the disoriented anger of the "separated" exec by offering him a chance to "ventilate" it. Within minutes after "separation" the executive is given a programmed opportunity to express his or her rage and shock—but only to a hired surrogate called an "outplacement" expert.

These procedures amount to acts of violence as premeditated as the gauntlet decreed by Nicholas I in Tolstoy's story.

As larger and more complex systems exert increasing control over people, sources of violence become harder to pinpoint. In *The Grapes of Wrath,* tenant farmers, about to be thrown off their land by owner men, try to comprehend their fate at the hands of impersonal sources.

> Sure, cried the tenant men, but it's our land. We measured it and broke it up. We were born on it, and we got killed on it, died on it. Even if it's no good, it's still ours. That's what makes it ours—being born on it, working it, dying on it. That makes ownership, not a paper with numbers on it.
>
> We're sorry. It's not us. It's the monster. The bank isn't like a man.
>
> Yes, but the bank is only made of men.
>
> No, you're wrong there—quite wrong there. The bank is something else than men. It happens that every man in a bank hates what the bank does, and yet the bank does it. The bank is something more than men, I tell you. It's the monster. Men made it, but they can't control it.
>
> The tenants cried, Grampa killed Indians, Pa killed snakes for the land. Maybe we can kill banks—they're worse than Indians and snakes. Maybe we got to fight to keep our land, like Pa and Grampa did.
>
> And now the owner men grew angry. You'll have to go.
>
> But it's ours, the tenant men cried. We——

No. The bank, the monster owns it. You'll have to go.
We'll get our guns, like Grampa when the Indians came.
What then?

It used to be much easier for people to point the finger at their
enemies and figure out the obstacles they faced. Life's chal-
lenges had many more predictable limits. People had a better
idea of who the bad guys were because the bad guys were most
often visible. Now "invisible forces" damage people. There's no
one to shoot. As a result, some people have cloistered themselves
in closed communities with strict rules and limits. With their
straightforward definitions, these communities, communes, or
cults offer a roster of clearly defined enemies. But most people
have opted to contain themselves as best they can, lowering their
expectations of "success" to make security their primary goal.
This seems to have happened either because they can't figure out
where the proverbial ladder to success is or because the ladder
they've been climbing keeps being pulled out from under them
(again by "invisible forces" for undefined reasons).

A few persons have reacted to the nebulous but pervasive
violence by taking up arms to shoot anybody, everybody, or
themselves.

What the people in the supermarket and I have in common
with the factory executive and the tenant farmers is the
impersonal violence we have to contend with but can't prevent or
confront. To varying degrees, control has been taken out of our
hands.

Progress in the land of the free has produced a nation of
victims—Black, Hispanic, Polish, Italian, Jewish, parent, child,
teacher, policeman, overtaxed middle class, overregulated upper
class, overscrutinized lower class—all vying for recognition.
More open competition exists over which group is considered the
most oppressed than over who ranks highest in the pecking
order. The victim has emerged as a hero, with a unique power
that comes with being an undisputed underdog.

When psychologist Alfred Adler described the phenomena of
the inferiority complex, he was referring to the basic state of

helplessness with which we are all born and which many people never overcome. Our empathy for the victim comes from these early feelings and is one of the few common threads left in our pluralistic society.

For years one of the most popular game shows on both radio and television capitalized on our sympathy for and empathy with the victim. *Queen for a Day* made the floors of America sopping wet with tears. Dapper Jack Bailey, the show's host, would introduce three women who were supposed to live in the most horrendous circumstances anyone could imagine. After each participant told of her tragedies (I hesitate to call them contestants, though that's what they were—people competing for prizes awarded to whoever the audience thought was closest to total ruination), Bailey would call on the audience to give the storyteller a round of applause. To thunderous clapping the weeping woman would leave the stage, only to return at the end of the show to see who had convinced the audience that she was the biggest loser. The biggest loser was, of course, the winner.

The final announcement, after America was reassured that three more wretches would be presented on the following day, was Jack Bailey's optimistic sign-off, "Remember, *you too* can be Queen For a Day."

Feeling powerless, people have become more preoccupied with the effect the world has on them than with the effect they could have on the world. This trend must have led President John F. Kennedy to plead prophetically and unsuccessfully with the youth of America, "Ask not what your country can do for you, but what you can do for your country." If people thought themselves capable of doing something for their country, they would be openly admitting to personal power and effectiveness. That would mean giving up the identity of the victim. In a society whose aid and sentiment is with the underdog, giving up that identity means giving up a great deal of influence.

By definition, helplessness excuses people from the responsibility of changing their lives or confronting the destructive forces that control them. People need to reject the *idea* of using violence and present themselves as victims of violence in order to remain underdogs. Meanwhile, under cover, they have developed subtle tactics to gain personal power.

As people have become obsessed with the active violence around them, *passive* violence has become more of a threat. People are focusing on active violence in the same way the northern states riveted their attention on the problems of segregation in the South during the fifties as a diversion from some other pressing problems closer to home. While turning into a *different kind* of violent animal, we are looking the other way—denying what we are becoming. The openly aggressive surge for power that once defined the American character is changing, and though we know little about the kinds of violence that clearly victimized so many in the past, we know even less about what our new identity implies for the future.

Between what we have been, with all our wars and murders and shootouts, and what we will become, I see us as a society of violent sheep, cornered and dangerous victims.

"Time, events, or the unaided individual action of the mind, will sometimes undermine or destroy an opinion without any outward sign of change," Alexis de Tocqueville wrote in *Democracy in America*. "It has not been openly assailed, no conspiracy has been formed to make war on it, but its followers one by one noiselessly secede; day by day a few of them abandon it, until at last it is only professed by a minority."

People are clinging to a narrow definition of violence as the nature of violence expands. The population pretends not to see what it knows is there.

Historians and anthropologists of the future will judge the success of our adaptive tactics. But, while going through changes in the way we live, however, we should take the wool from our eyes and see what violence has become.

Passive Violence

Individuals are passively but persistently bombarded from "above." Ironically, most attacks on people come from the systems and institutions that were designed to protect them.

In his book *Mind Control*, Peter Schrag explains how we are quietly but efficiently provoked and controlled by "invisible forces" that intrude on our lives:

> . . . the technologies and disciplines associated with apparently benevolent social objectives—and particularly the social and behavioral sciences—could, we discovered, be turned handily to the purposes of pacification, intimidation, obfuscation, propaganda, and war; could be used just as easily for control as for liberation; and could serve for mystification as readily as they could serve for enlightenment.
>
> What we missed is the extent to which private organizations and the "benign" branches of government—universities, foundations, employers, credit bureaus, schools, the National Institute of Mental Health, the U. S. Office of Education, the Department of Health, Education, and Welfare, and local and state welfare agencies—were, and are, in the business of surveillance and behavior control; the extent to which a police mentality, social welfare attitudes of "service," and medical model "therapy" have fused; and the extent to which a substantial part—if not the majority—of the population has been taught to accept those impositions as routine. . . .

More than one hundred and fifty years after Czar Nicholas I, our institutions have developed the art of anti-violent violence (how many wars and weapons have been called "deterrents"?), non-violent cruelty (a "non-punitive," medically accepted treatment for modifying young bedwetters' behavior involved hanging the soiled bedsheet out the window as a "reminder"), and of passively inflicted pain (the labels "culturally deprived" and "educationally disadvantaged" have been hung around the necks of children who carry them as lifelong brandings of failure).

* * *

Poet Karl Shapiro observes, "Betrayal is an act of vengeance, obviously. But in an age of betrayal, when men of authority traduce their office and violate the trust placed in their hands, betrayal becomes the 'official morality.' " He continues: " 'Official morality' shortly becomes 'public immorality'; whereupon the fabric of a society rots before one's eyes. In the years since the end of the Second World War, announced by the drop of the first Ultimate Weapon, the world has been stunned, horrified, and ultimately cajoled and won over to the official morality of America and its corollary of public immorality and anarchy. Hardly a leader, whether President, general, public-relations man, professor, publisher, or poet, can be held to be honorable in his intentions."

We copy the violence imposed on us by our benevolent institutions. It becomes a model for the way we impose ourselves in personal relationships. Few people understand the *subtle* ways institutions oppress them. Even fewer make the connection between this organized oppression and their own control and manipulation of others.

One group's bad guy is another group's hero. Since no one wants to see himself as a bad guy, groups deny, distort, and rationalize the cruelty they feel they have to inflict. The KKK and Communists, bosses and workers, union leaders and government reformers have one common bond. They all have elaborate rationalizations for the means they use to their ends. Almost everyone needs to see himself as rational, good, and peaceloving.

Shifting the responsibility for violence may be one of the few common bonds among all of us, from Nazi to humanist, terrorist to pacifist. The degree of violence we cover up may be significantly different, but the process is the same. We justify and deny.

One of the more effective ways to justify violence is for persons to convince themselves that they are even greater victims than the persons they are victimizing. Most of the violence of "true believers" is justified this way. By amplifying their own oppression, people can persuade themselves to do almost anything to anyone.

Two nonviolent friends of mine are in the midst of a nasty

divorce. They feel victimized by each other and have justified all the abuse they practice by saying that they're "just getting back" at the other for abuse that has been inflicted upon them. They also deny their own violence either by not recognizing what they're doing or by saying the violence they've done hasn't been intentional. They are both taking defensive stands in order to justify their offenses.

He's put her car in a repair shop and won't tell her which one. But he says he's "only trying to get the thing fixed." In retaliation she's hidden his golf clubs and has confiscated some of his personal papers because "that's the only way I'm going to get my car back."

Most of their combat isn't so easily identifiable. It's covert. Knowing one another as well as they do makes it easy to attack while pretending innocence.

She has a serious chronic disease that flares up with stress. As their relationship has deteriorated she has become nearly bedridden. The more sick she is the more he yells that her illness is just "something you're doing to yourself." Knowing that he sleeps late and is easily awakened, she, who is not otherwise a compulsive housekeeper, is keeping house loudly, early in the morning. When he jumps out of bed screaming, she explains, "With all this tension I need something to do." Each has taken to lapsing into long periods of strategic silences that drive the other crazy.

Only a few years ago this couple would have used a popular official excuse for divorce. It was called "mental cruelty," a legal definition of passive violence. Now the law is more liberal. People can get "no-fault" divorces. Outwardly these divorces may seem more amiable; at least they are cheaper for the couple. But "no-fault" is just legal language. Fault and blame still exist in ruptured marriages, although they may be expressed passively. The language has been changed to protect the image of the innocent.

Passive violence carried out by someone convinced of his or her supremacy as a victim is an effective and dangerous weapon in daily victim-to-victim combat. The ultimate victim becomes the victor.

*   *   *

Dictionary definitions of violence are based on intent and apparent action. The *Random House College Dictionary* defines violence as "an unjust or unwarranted exertion of force or power." This may cover the more classical assaults and invasions but doesn't deal with the passive violence of manipulation and inaction. Our definition of violence should be broadened to take the covert variety into account. The dictionary definition does not explain what is "unjust and unwarranted." Is that determined by the aggressor? The victim? Or do we have to count on a third party to make that decision?

One of the problems that middle-class parents see in school integration is that their kids aren't as tough as poor kids. They're afraid that the poor kids are going to clobber their relatively defenseless children. These fears are backed up by newspaper stories about middle-class kids being attacked in bathrooms or on their way home from school. The fear of the middle-class parent is not unfounded.

But I've seen the other side of the problem, which is not so well reported. The covert violence perpetrated unknowingly by middle-class kids may be causing many of the unsubtle reactions of the poor. Since the middle-class children don't even realize what they're doing, it's a big problem, a part of the integration problem no one is talking about.

For a while I led "group rap" sessions in a high school that had just been integrated. In one of the marathon sessions, Seth, a new middle-class white student, squeaked out to Carlos, a second-year, poor Puerto Rican student, "I'm afraid of you." According to Seth, Carlos seemed violent. Carlos, who wanted to be an artist (at the time he was drawing cartoon figures of Nixon with an Afro haircut), had been feeling "vibes" from Seth and wanted to know what he meant. Seth told Carlos in a very quiet, roundabout way that Carlos's full Afro made him look wild, that the way Carlos dressed made Seth uptight, and that Carlos raised his voice a lot.

"So what can I do?" Carlos sincerely wanted to know. This was Carlos's attempt to be racially tolerant. (He had told me before school began that he was going to try to "understand about other people.") "What can I do?" he repeated.

Seth didn't really answer Carlos. He told Carlos that everything Carlos was, said, and stood for was a threat, and that he couldn't get over his fear until Carlos changed. But it took several hours to get this information out in the open, and, by the time it came out, Carlos had worked harder than I had ever seen him work at trying to understand the message between the lines.

The wear and tear on Carlos was visible and he began showing signs of suppressed rage. The more impatient he became, the more outspoken Seth became. Finally, after Carlos couldn't stand it anymore and responded with a loud outburst, Seth did a "See, I told you" to the group. This eroded the final bit of patience Carlos had. He challenged Seth to a fight.

"See I told you. See, I told you. . . ."

But the group's tolerance had ebbed in the three-hour session. We had seen more than Seth had wanted us to see. We had seen Seth goad and push Carlos into the role Seth wanted to confirm.

There was no fight. No one was hurt physically. But the minute Carlos became the violent Puerto Rican Seth wanted him to be, Carlos lost.

"How did this happen to me?" Carlos asked the group. People who had been following the whole thing closely explained what they saw. And Carlos understood. But he never talked to Seth again.

"Those middle-class guys can sure eat up your mind." Carlos was much stronger than Seth but he was afraid.

"I didn't mean anything personally," Seth said later. "I was just trying to work out the problem and communicate."

The people best adapted to our culture have become experts in the passive violence they've learned from their social institutions. They have learned the moves and actions necessary to disarm an adversary, just as a boxer or karate expert knows how to move in open combat. The actively violent are exposed and vulnerable. The passively violent escape detection or retaliation by hiding behind philosophies, words, or even just facial expressions to cover their intent.

Since there are so many ways violent intent can be disowned, violence should instead be defined by its *effect*. The definition should include any act that makes a person or group of people feel hurt, angry, despondent, helpless, violent, or apathetic, by using words, phrases, or concepts to throw off balance or disarm the person's defenses.

When you know you've been hurt or made uncomfortable but you don't know what hit you, you've probably been victimized by some sort of passive violence.

THE WHOOPS FACTOR

One very successful way to obscure violence is by understanding and invoking the Whoops Factor. It is a favorite means of denying violence and is used at all levels from the closest of relationships to global politics. It can be a rational excuse for unintended violence or it can be a smokescreen for directed, covert violence.

It is expressed in four basic phrases that, in barbershop harmony, could become our new national anthem. They are:

"I didn't mean it."
"Don't take it personally."
"Anyone can make a mistake."
"It seemed like a good idea at the time."

The essential message is innocence. Saying "whoops" denies responsibility and motive. But its primary goal is to eliminate the possibility that a given act might be *interpreted* as violent.

When used intentionally, the Whoops Factor can turn an act of violence inside out and make the attacker seem like a victim. This often provokes open, active violence in unsuspecting prey.

The Whoops Factor has excused everything from passing gas in a crowded room to the bombing of noncombatant villages in wartime. Some people say it will be responsible for the end of the world.

One morning I heard a loud banging noise under my house and went down to see what was the matter. The noise came from a wrench applied to a gas pipe, and, as I got to the hatch that opened onto the gas meter, I saw a uniformed representative of the gas company making the last few turns of the wrench.

I asked him what he was doing and he told me that he was there to turn off the gas. He said the bill hadn't been paid and he had spent some time ringing the doorbell, but when no one answered he had decided that no one was home and set about turning off the gas. In the process, he had loosened some pipes, he warned, but that wasn't his problem any more, since the gas was off. When it was turned on, he said, I should make sure the crew fixed the loosened pipes.

I was surprised and annoyed to find he was there to turn off the gas for nonpayment when the bill had long since been paid.

"Really?" he asked. "Do you have a receipt?"

I got the receipt, which was dated three weeks earlier.

"Jesus," he said, "if I would'a seen this, I never would'a turned off your gas."

"Well," I said patiently, "now you have seen it. Will you please turn it back on?"

"I can't *do* that," he countered, as if I should have known that I was asking the impossible. "I only turn the gas off. There's another crew that has to come and turn it on."

"But you have the same wrench you used to turn it off and you know exactly what you did. Why don't you just start from what you did last and work backwards?"

I had missed the point. He looked at me as if I had just landed from Mars.

"It wasn't *my* mistake. The company has your name down here on my list for turnoff for nonpayment. Isn't your name Dennis?"

"No, my name is not Dennis and there is no Dennis here. You have the wrong address or the wrong person and I don't have the time to work out your company's problems. Right now I can't even make myself a cup of coffee."

"Jesus. They sure made a serious mistake. Do you have a phone?"

The gas man called the company and got someone on the other end who not only didn't understand what had happened, but, according to him, didn't really understand the serious liability the gas company had assumed by sending him to turn off the gas of someone who had obviously paid her bill. They said they would send a turn-on crew as soon as possible. The gas man, now an ally of mine, emphasized that this should be an "A-1" call, meaning first priority, because it was due to company error. The woman on the other end was new and didn't know what he meant. The gas man left after speaking to a supervisor, who reassured him that it would be considered an "A-1" call and that a crew would be there within an hour.

I waited.

After three hours, I called the gas company. I was angry. I had been promised that everything would be back to normal within an hour, yet I was still waiting. The woman I spoke to wasn't the least bit concerned with what her company had done, who was being inconvenienced, or anything else. Most of all, she couldn't understand my "impatience."

"After all," she said, "we're running shorthanded. We don't have enough crews to answer all the calls. You can't expect us to be everywhere at once. Besides, anyone can make a mistake."

All of a sudden I was transformed. I was no longer the victim of someone's bungling, which had invaded my privacy and disrupted my day. I was, instead, the one who was victimizing the gas company, making unreasonable demands and abusing this innocent employee, who, she reminded me, "wasn't the one who turned it off in the first place."

The game had gone something like this:

The man who turned the gas off tried to rouse me first, but I didn't hear the bell—Whoops.

So he turned off my gas, which he wouldn't have done if he had seen my receipt beforehand, or if the company hadn't made the mistake in the first place—Whoops.

Then he couldn't turn it on, because "that's not my job"—Whoops.

The crew he called that would be there within an hour didn't show up after three hours—Whoops.

And when I called to complain about all of this, *I* ended up an unreasonable person who doesn't understand the problems of a big organization that is doing its best against impossible odds. By not understanding their position, I have become another one of *their* obstacles. They feel victimized by me.

I'm angry, but there's no one to be angry *at*. Everyone is blameless, except, as it turns out, me.

"We'll have someone there as soon as we can," the woman at the gas company said condescendingly, then added, "Have a nice day."

When the crew showed up four hours late to turn on the gas, turn on the various pilot lights, and recheck all the connections, they were comforting.

"This happens all the time. Don't take it personally," said the chief. "Have a nice day," he said as he left.

It was noon, four hours after the banging under the house had disturbed me. And I felt as if I'd been robbed.

In the movie *Dr. Strangelove,* a crazy commander of a Strategic Air Command base carefully plans a sneak attack on the Russians. He launches the attack of bombers loaded with nuclear weapons and protects against their recall by killing himself to make it impossible for anyone to find the recall code before the bombers reach their Soviet targets.

When the President and Joint Chiefs of Staff find out about this, they try to stop the aircraft by sending out fighters to shoot them down and giving top secret technical information to Russian missile bases to make sure that none of the bombers get through.

But one does get through and it's clear that it is going to drop its bomb on a Russian target.

The President calls the Russian prime minister. He tells him what has happened and what is about to happen. He offers his apologies, making it clear that he did everything he could to prevent this, but now. . . .

The Russian prime minister is not impressed. How does he know that this whole thing isn't a trick? He's going to have to retaliate.

"But, Dimitri," says the President, "we didn't mean it. I mean, look, Dimitri, anyone can make a mistake. You're not being reasonable, Dimitri."

Anyone *can* make a mistake. And in that reality lies the safety of the Whoops Factor which makes it the most effective passively violent tactic. Not only can you not fight a mistake, you'll be running in circles if you try.

The Whoops Factor can result in your best friend "accidentally" staining a new shirt you were just about to wear to an important interview, a member of a surprise party "inadvertently" tipping off the subject, someone "forgetting" to give you an urgent message, or someone calling you on the phone early Sunday morning when he knows it's the only morning you can sleep late. Whether or not these acts are intentional, the person they affect feels victimized and helpless to say anything to the victimizer.

Justice Oliver Wendell Holmes said that even a dog distinguishes between being stumbled over and being kicked. Somehow we are losing our animal instincts, our ability to sniff out an aggressor.

That ability to spot, label, and respond to an aggressor is lost in the backwash of relativism. Absolute values are nonexistant, unreasonable, out of touch, unrealistic. We have come to understand the reasons and explanations for our own destruction as if they make us less vulnerable.

"What we have here," said the prison farm boss in the movie *Cool Hand Luke,* as he turned to the road gang after beating Luke senseless for his persistent non-conformity "is a failure to communicate."

Violent Passivity

In a conversation with Martin Luther King, Albert Einstein said, "The world is too dangerous to live in. Not because of the people who do violence but because of the people who sit by and let it happen."

Violent passivity is another expression of violence. Unlike passive violence, which substitutes covert tactics for open aggression (using passivity as a cover for attack), violently passive people indulge, feed off, and, by their inaction, even comply with violence without appearing to be associated with it.

In the fifties a group of magazine photographers were sent to cover a French nuclear blast on a small atoll. After the blast, the photographers were permitted to shoot some pictures of the weapon's effect. They noticed that the sea turtles that normally laid their eggs in the sand were disoriented and were laying their eggs in the wrong direction, so that they drifted en masse out into the ocean, assuring that they would not survive.

The photographers carefully documented this terrible side effect of atomic energy, noting that they were recording the end of the life cycle of an entire species. Turtles that swam hundreds, maybe thousands, of miles to lay their eggs on this particular island were now disoriented and were, in effect, performing their own last rites. It was a dramatic story, not only because of the plight of the turtles, but because not one photographer turned a single turtle around towards the sand. They watched and they clicked. They didn't do any violence. They simply detached themsleves from it and allowed it to happen.

Twenty years later a television film crew was accused of staging a gang fight while filming the documentary, "Youth Terror: The View From Behind the Gun." Actually, the members of the crew had not staged the fight but did know beforehand about the plans for it. They just didn't see it as their business to "intrude." They got important footage for their documentary while many of the young people they were filming were seriously injured. The film crew and production people were indignant that anyone would accuse them of having anything to do with the violence. All they did, they said, was "observe and film."

Television itself helps make most people violently passive, despite the claims in a few notorious legal cases like *Niemi* vs. *NBC* in San Francisco and the Zamora case in Florida, each of which accused television programs of motivating the active violence of several young defendants.

In the Niemi case, a young girl sued NBC after she was raped by a group of girls with a broom handle. This same kind of assault had been shown in an NBC television movie about a girls' reform school. The case was based on the plaintiff's assumption that her attackers watched the movie and were compelled somehow to imitate the violence they saw on the screen.

The Zamora case involved a young man who accused television of fomenting his own violence against a woman who had caught him robbing her house. Zamora claimed he was only imitating a character he had seen on television the night before.

Both were landmark cases in that they were the first to blame violence on the suggestive effects of the video image. Both cases lost in the lower courts, but their importance lies in the willingness of a large number of people, including organizations like the PTA, to blame television for inciting violence.

Television doesn't create active violence. It teaches people to observe it in the same way they watch commercials— dispassionately. To separate oneself from the emotional suffering of another is a way of depersonalizing violence, and I have no doubt that television helps people do this. It doesn't program them to inflict suffering but to accept and tolerate it, to become passive spectators of the violence around them.

In the search for peace of mind in a culture where information about everyone's problems intrudes upon us daily, we have become skilled in disavowing responsibility for anything outside our tiny islands of acknowledged competence or interest.

Freedom has become freedom *from:* from having to look at unpleasantness or from having to deal with problems. Freedom has come to mean calling on surrogates or specialists to take problems away.

This is fairly easy to do in a society in which people are cast in narrow roles (doctor, blue collar, social worker, anti-abortionist, liberal, and so on). There is no cohesive whole to which people can be responsible, but only a collection of roles and categories that each person sees as relevant to himself. General social responsibility has become an abstraction. Violent passivity has become a norm.

"Looking the other way" has become a chronic problem in every field. In the practice of medicine it is an especially dramatic threat. The doctors and hospital administrators in New York who allowed surgical salesmen to assist in over nine hundred surgical operations were violently passive. So were the hospital personnel who permitted sterilizations of women on welfare, knowing the women had not been informed of the nature of their operations. Doctors, hospitals, nurses, medical groups, and insurance companies who refuse to tell the public about incompetent colleagues (exposing the public to incalculable amounts of suffering and damage) are all violently passive.

"Streamers," GI's who went to their deaths in unopened parachutes (many of which their manufacturers knew to be defective), were casualties of violent passivity. Children who have died of "child abuse" because no one thought it was his business to intrude upon family brutality died as much from violent passivity as from the abuse. The innocent people who are dead because a friend didn't think it was his or her place to interfere with a drunkard's desire to drive home are victims of the violently passive.

Most people don't want to be "intrusive." Using "legitimate" or even moral reasons ("I won't deny your right to your decision to. . . ."), we passively license violence.

Freddy Prinze was a comedian whose routine included a segment in which he told of his experiences with a building janitor he knew. In this segment the custodian would deliver one response whenever anyone in the building asked him to do something: "It's not my job, man." It was a line that got instant recognition from an overspecialized, bureaucratized people.

Prinze died by putting a gun to his head and pulling the trigger. Friends and his psychiatrist knew he had threatened suicide before, had even made the same gesture with the same weapon that ultimately killed him. A day before his death, Prinze had given his gun to his psychiatrist. When he asked for its return, the psychiatrist complied. The psychiatrist explained after Freddy's death that his patient was an adult and the gun couldn't be kept against the patient's wishes. The psychiatrist wasn't, after all, in the storage business, nor was he about to take responsibility for the life of his patient. Ironically, he assumed Prinze's comic character, simply saying, "It's not my job, man."

Violent passivity is an eerie thing. It represents a missing link in our connections to one another, a flaw that cuts off empathy and lets us passively observe what we might actively prevent.

Being numbed to violence and skilled in denying it, we allow much more cruelty than we admit. We've accepted the childish sense of safety that wishes bad things away by simply closing the eyes. But sooner or later we open them and find that the world is going about its business as usual. While we weren't looking, we became easy prey. Now, we may cry out for help. But no one else is looking, either.

Biological Determinism

Both passive violence and violent passivity have physiological as well as cultural implications. Coping with rapid changes in our society has strained our biological adaptability as well as our intellectual capacity. All our strategies of personal survival are hooked into automatic physical responses we may not be aware of. Regardless of how well we *think*, our body is still geared to respond to dangers and attacks that our intellect may interpret as "safe."

Even at our civilized best, making clever conversation and meeting new people at obligatory cocktail parties, a part of us still looks out for saber-toothed tigers and dangerous enemies with sharpened sticks. The primitive human instincts have not gone away. They are there with us as we smile over mai-tais wishing we were someplace else.

Primitive man didn't face as many subtly violent situations as civilized man does. He either killed an enemy or got away before he could be killed—it was fight or flight.

Whatever primitive man did, whether foraging alone or working in some kind of cooperative way, his senses were keyed to self-defense. When his brain signaled danger he didn't take a whole lot of time pondering the situation. It was red alert.

Pushing the panic button released into the bloodstream a flood of hormones that increased strength and speed. The hypothalamus sent electrochemical signals down through the body to the endocrine system. That system released adrenalin and noradrenalin. It was pretty much the same biological response we have today when we hear a noise at the door late at night. Adrenalin activates the liver. Glucose, liberated and distributed throughout the body, provides immediate muscular energy and euphoric strength while allowing greater performance from the heart and lungs. If things are bad enough, noradrenalin activates free fatty acids to help muscles work even harder (and also to make blood thicken to facilitate rapid clotting in case of injury).

It is a perfect system as long as the emergency energy, once

23

triggered, is spent by fighting or running. But now the system is outdated. We don't respond to all the serious signals our adrenal glands receive by looking to kill or by running away. Our understanding of events has become more complex. But our primitive system, with all its sensors and its on-off switch, is still intact.

In some ways it's good to have it with us as an emergency system. Who knows when a one-hundred-twenty-pound woman will have to pull a two-thousand-pound car off her husband? But for the most part our bodies are like super-horsepowered engines. They may be impressive but they consume a lot of unnecessary energy, cause internal pollution, and have a lot of breakdowns. Progress, as usual, has brought a mixed bag of pleasures and problems.

People have difficulties with their fight-flight response and its related sensory radar. The problems date back to the development of the neocortex, the beginning of man's capacity to bypass anger in favor of moral law or social contracts. Complex societies brought with them pressures to *avoid* violence for the common good. Anger was transformed from a trigger for action, the finger on the panic button, to a substitute for action. The fight-flight response was now defused by the thought of consequences. When the primitive biological response began to conflict with new laws and contracts agreed to by the neocortex, the nervous system's compromise was repressed rage and anger without action. Being stuck with a primitive alarm system in a sophisticated social network is really a bad evolutionary joke.

As human response to attack evolved from reflexive action into thought, people also became capable of deliberate, planned violence unaccompanied by massive chemical flows. Occasionally, in extreme stress or danger, instinctive violence could override reason and people would be subject to fits of rage, "seeing red," and would generally raise hell and wreak havoc, just as in those days when they were climbing around on the rocks. But, more often, signals to attack were overridden by their "higher centers" and they would stand back and think, and decide that action wasn't worth it, after all. People could do subtler violence within the existing morality or social agreements. Moreover, they could do so without being hit by a hormonal storm.

The primitive and civilized capacities of the human brain are in constant struggle. This psycho-biological odd couple causes a lot of confusion in body chemistry. While our primitive instincts look out for trouble, our thought processes are working on that information, fitting our responses to the social codes we have accepted. We repress instinct in favor of the social contract. We agree to moral laws like "Thou shalt not kill." We say, "I won't do this, if you won't do that." Whatever our cultural contracts, however, the brain still can pick up what it considers to be a danger signal and "send in the troops" without hesitating.

In this age of anxiety we live in a world that impinges on us at every turn. Our neocortex is working overtime to mediate our primitive instincts. In a state of nearly constant alert, our system that once dealt effectively with outside threats has turned into a threat of its own.

Instead of driving us to run away or fight an enemy, the chemical energy triggered by anger sits in our bodies—a deadly residue. To an "illogical" endocrine system, cut loose by primitive triggers, we become our own enemy, our own victim.

Every time a person is aroused to anger and doesn't translate the resulting neurological and endocrine impulses into action, the body responds with a chemical flow that, instead of stimulating muscle and heart action, releases acid into the stomach and fatty acids into the blood vessels—the roots of ulcers and atherosclerosis.

Enter "the victim." Victimization complicates matters, turning an already dangerous biochemical collision into a social and political nightmare. Feeling chronically victimized is like placing nitroglycerine in the hands of a potential terrorist: an unevolved neurophysiology combines with complex justifications for violence.

Douglas Colligan, writing in *New York* magazine, examines the combination of stress and helplessness.

In 1957 Dr. Curt Richter, a Johns Hopkins psychologist, drowned two wild rats. He dropped Rat One into a tank of warm water, and since rats are generally pretty good swimmers, it lasted for about sixty hours before finally becoming exhausted and drowning. With Rat Two he tried something different. Before releasing it in the water, he held it in his hand until it stopped struggling. Once he dropped it into the tank, it splashed around for a few minutes, then passively sank to the bottom. Richter claims that Rat Two had despaired of escape even before it got wet, and, in effect, died of helplessness. In those years that have passed since those rats drowned, an impressive pile of evidence has accumulated showing us that there's a little of Rat Two in each of us.[1]

Feeling chronically helpless and victimized seems to make us even more vulnerable to self-defeating behavior than our archaic biochemical predispositions alone. It may be some time, if we decide to give ourselves time, before we can sort out how much our victim mentality creates helplessness as predictable as that in Rat Two, how much it adds to our potential for violence, and how much, as human beings, we can really overcome.

Victimization is everywhere: too much television, not enough love, too many food additives, not enough vitamins, too much violence, not enough leadership, too permissive teachers, not enough freedom. All these and other oppressions have created an unpleasant and elusive flock of personalities I call Violent Sheep.

The incongruity of the words "violent" and "sheep" is intentional and implies deception. They represent the two most active forces in these personalities. The violence, expressed passively for reasons already discussed but still to be elaborated, is exerted to establish control. The term sheep exemplifies anonymity and conformity, both primary traits of this creature.

Violent Sheep have been bred to react, not to act. To respond, not to initiate. To trust no one, including themselves. They deny

[1]The research is significant on a number of levels, not the least of which is why Dr. Richter allowed the rats to drown once it was clear they weren't going to stay afloat. The Rat One and Rat Two research may also be pointing out a Rat Three—Dr. Richter's passive, depersonalized violence. (They were, after all, just "wild rats" who had served their purpose.)

responsibility but seek out sources of blame. They would rather be experts than leaders, dependent than loyal.

They have been taught that appearance is more important than substance, that nothing is certain, that there are no answers. There is no absolute right or wrong, good or evil. Under the fleece they have only a learned set of responses to the moment. They are judged by ever present "invisible juries" (a phrase coined by writer Joseph Rosner) who invariably bring in verdicts of guilty, confirming their feelings of helplessness and futility and justifying their continued passive assaults.

They are, these Violent Sheep, our new aggressors, affecting our everyday life in small ways and, more substantially, our future as a people and a society.

What follows is a look into the ways Violent Sheep affect our routine behavior.

II

Our New Aggressors
The Flock

The Flock is the collective of Violent Sheep. It comprises the actions and reactions that support passively violent personalities. In its broadest sense, the Flock symbolizes every social group's tendency toward conformity and control through covert tactics.

The purpose of this section is to examine some of the most common passively violent actions and to describe some of the personality types who perform them. Since much of the Flock's malignant effect lies in its ability to inflict violence and escape discovery, awareness of its patterns of behavior is the most obvious way to minimize or even prevent its destructiveness.

The personalities that follow come from real life. We often ignore them as they create undercurrents or provoke open expressions of violence. Their innocent or benign appearance makes their violence passive. The active violence we can see, identify, and understand is easier to defend against. Passive violence has evolved precisely because it resists effective defense. I hope to create some greater immunity to that resistant strain of violence by describing a few members of the Flock.

Many of the scenes presented here may be subject to interpretations of intent—that is, they may appear to involve "errors of judgment," "accidents," "mistakes," or "misunderstandings." Only educated judgment can ultimately differentiate the innocent acts from their passively violent counterparts. These judgments are based on frequency, predictability, and severity of the "errors." Though passive violence is usually a consistent series of well masked acts that inflict pain and discomfort on their targets again and again, it can also be expressed in a single act that is not so well masked.

I'm reading a newspaper while standing in a long line at the post office. The man behind me clears his throat and says, "Excuse me, but do you have a pen? I have to address my letter."

"Sure," I say, and fumble with the newspaper while digging through my purse to find my pen.

The man takes the pen, addresses his letter, and gives it back to me.

"You got any change?" He's trading the pen for the next favor. "I gotta make a call and all I've got are quarters."

I dig back in my purse and find change for a quarter.

"Hey, thanks. Will you keep my place in line?"

I barely nod yes and go back to reading the paper. A couple of minutes later the man's back. He clears his throat and taps me lightly. "You got the time?"

"Oh, man." I sigh as I look at my watch. Before I have the chance to tell him the time he snarls, "Hey, lady, you don't have to get so huffy about it."

From a psychologist's viewpoint, this man has problems of dependency But diagnostic explanations don't help me as a victim. One hundred psychologists may give me one hundred reasons why this person intrudes, irritates, and provokes me as he does. An equal number of gurus may give me an infinite number of ways to ignore or immunize myself from such behavior. But I'm concerned here with classifying and identifying passively violent or violently passive acts. I'm not concerned with the many ways we have learned or could learn to tolerate and absorb them. Passively violent people depend upon their victims' indulgence.

The following character descriptions do not deal with excuses or explanations for the Violent Sheep's destructive behavior. I am interested only in exposing the kinds of violence that make us feel victimized, put upon, and outraged, and strengthen our common tendency to be other victims' Violent Sheep.

AUTHOR'S NOTE
In the following introductions and descriptions of the Flock, I have used the masculine pronouns "he" and "his" rather than the more cumbersome "he or she" and "his or her." I have chosen this abbreviation for clarity and consistency, not to imply that all passively violent characters are male.

The Crisis Monger

The Crisis Monger is never there when you need him. His crisis is always bigger, more important, and more threatening than anyone else's. His expectations of other people are monumental and demand attention. When the time comes for him to reciprocate, however, his only response is a bigger and better personal crisis. He is always preoccupied and helpless but still tries to give the impression that he's interested in close relationships—if he could only solve *this* crisis.

The Crisis Monger puts himself in center stage, making constant demands of the people around him and never paying his dues. He skillfully wins the support of others with promises of friendship and loyalty that he never keeps and never expects to because the Crisis Monger is in a constant state of oppression.

The Crisis Monger creates problems to escape personal or social responsibilities. Once a part of the Crisis Monger's following, a person must be always available, never demanding, and unendingly sympathetic. Violators are publicly vilified as "unfeeling," "unreasonable," and "selfish."

Crisis Mongers may briefly become leaders of cults or social protest groups, when their ability to mobilize in their own behalf is misperceived as an ability to sustain support for a group or cause. Since all their energies ultimately center around themselves, their mistaken followers are quickly disillusioned.

CRISIS MONGER I

Born and brought up in Watts, Harry didn't have much of a chance at the California dream. His life, like many others, could easily be found as a case study in a social work journal. No father. Welfare. All five brothers and sisters dropouts. And Harry, the youngest, heading for the streets with the same unfocused determination as the rest of his family.

What wasn't written up in any of the journals was Harry's devotion to his mother. She was a pleasant woman who always seemed to be trying her best, which, unfortunately, was not good enough. She always needed something. It wasn't only Harry who tried to protect her; his brothers and sisters did also. Since none of them had "done good," mama was the victim of their inadequacy. Each of their failures became her failure to be able to do enough for them. She was so wounded by their problems and tragedies that her children had learned to keep their disappointments from her.

Harry was the most sensitive to his mother's plight. He had determined that if he ever got into terrible trouble he would leave the family forever to protect mama from the bad boy he knew he really was.

Sure enough, like the rest of his family, Harry was picked up for truancy one day.Finding a sizeable amount of marijuana on him, the police tossed him into a detention center before deciding what to do with him.

Out in a day, Harry didn't want to go home, didn't ever want to see his mother again for fear of causing her more trouble. He climbed a fire escape on the tallest building on his block (a four story, gerry-built thing). Waiting for only a small crowd to gather, Harry jumped to the street.

Within minutes the whole block was filled with shrieks and screams. People ran to Harry's apartment to get his mother while Harry lay motionless on the pavement.

Mama ran out of her building, hands in the air, squealing and crying. Her two daughters were right behind her. One son ran across the street to meet her, and they all ran towards Harry.

But before they reached him, mama fainted. She just dissolved right there in the middle of the street, only twenty yards from Harry. The brothers and sisters were frantic. "Mama!" they screamed. "Help! Won't somebody help?" they begged the crowd that had assembled around Harry's limp form.

The crowd, a little bewildered, ran toward Harry's mother— leaving Harry alone in the middle of the street—to see what all the screaming was about.

Mama couldn't be revived. Women ran into their apartments to get cold water for her forehead, others looked for spirits of ammonia. Finally, the two daughters got down on their knees and started to pray. Half the crowd followed their example, wailing and swaying in prayer.

Almost ten minutes later, a bruised figure crawled through the crowd towards mama.

"Don't die," Harry prayed by her side. "Don't die, mama."

Mama miraculously opened one eye. Her son was with her. Her crisis was over.

CRISIS MONGER II

"It's great to know real people," Mort is quick to point out, "people you can *count on,* people who *care.*" He means it and Jerry feels good that he has a friend who has an unusual willingness to put into words what most people silently accept. It's been nice to have Mort as a friend. He's always been open about what he wanted: to hang out with his pals, to set aside times to "do the joints," and to just be together with good people.

One day Jerry is feeling stuck and "blue," so he calls Mort and says "Hey, let's go hang out someplace. I could really use the break. How about going to Reggie's Grove? Haven't been there in a long time."

"Jeez, man, I'd love to, but Mona and I are having another 'thing' and this one's pretty heavy and I'm totally messed up about it. You think *you* could use a break, lemme tell you, I'd do *anything* just to get the hell out of here. But I've really gotta stay and work this thing out. I mean, it's really serious this time. I don't know what the hell I'm gonna do."

For thirty minutes Jerry listens to Mort talk about himself, retelling problems that Jerry has heard before, but this time they seem to have more disastrous implications than they've ever had. The conversation ends with Mort saying, "It's good to talk to you, man. You're always such a help. When I get things together here we'll—"

"Hey, man," Jerry interrupts, "this isn't the time to talk about us getting together."

The next week Jerry gets a call from Ron, a mutual friend of his and Mort's.

"We've gotta get Mort out of the house," Ron tells Jerry. "He really sounds like he's completely against the wall this time. I've got tickets to the concert tonight, and since you live closer to him than I do, why don't you pick him up? We can get him away from his problems for a few hours, anyway."

"Sure," says Jerry, "that's a good idea."

Jerry calls, tells Mort about the concert, and offers to pick him up.

"Hey, man, that's really fine," Mort responds. "It's really nice to know a guy has friends. I'll see you at seven."

When Jerry arrives at seven, Mort's not home. Jerry waits about an hour and leaves, worried that something might have happened or that maybe he wasn't clear about the arrangements. When he gets to the concert hall he looks for Mort but doesn't see him. Jerry decides to go in. He has Mort's ticket held for him at the box office. Inside, he spots Mort with some people Jerry's never seen before. He's not even with Ron, who originally called Jerry about the tickets. Ron's sitting in the seat next to Jerry.

"What the hell happened with Mort? Jesus, I called him and told him I'd pick him up at seven and he wasn't even home. What's going on?" Without waiting for an answer Jerry continues, "I'm going to find out," as he gets up from his seat.

"Look," Ron interrupts, pulling him back into his seat. "You know Mort, he's got so much on his head he probably doesn't even know what day it is."

"Yeah," Jerry readily agrees, feeling a little guilty now. "With Mona . . ."

"Mona?" Ron questions. "Oh, naw, he's not having any more trouble there. No. He's tangled in some big lawsuit that's got him crazy."

"Oh, God, not something else. . . ." Jerry sighs as the music begins.

At intermission Mort greets his two friends with a big hug and then pulls back, his mouth open. "Oh, hey. I was supposed to meet you guys someplace, wasn't I?"

"Well, yeah, you were," Jerry ventures. "I was by your place to pick you up."

"Boy, am *I* screwed up! Some friend I am, right?" He readily apologizes and then starts to explain. "Since this lawsuit came up—"

"We understand," Ron volunteers, before Mort has to do any more explaining.

"One of these days I'll get myself together."

"Forget about the mixup. You're under a lot of pressure. Just forget it."

"Hey, guys, I'll talk to you next week and we'll get together," Mort says as he drifts back to his seat and the house lights dim.

This isn't the first time something like this has happened with Mort. Jerry and Mort have been close friends since they worked in the same office together right out of college. Mort had always been the freer spirit of the two, but at the same time he had a lot more problems that needed attention. Jerry wasn't the only friend who had to pull him out of scrapes. Others of Mort's friends assumed the same role. Jerry never really thought to blame Mort for his problems. The problems were always out of Mort's control. He seemed to be a magnet for crazy landlords, demanding girl friends, drivers backing into him—all kinds of unusual things. Some of the problems were even funny. In fact, part of what made Mort interesting to Jerry were his problems, his crazy stories.

While Jerry listens to the music he thinks that this time he's going to stay away from Mort for a while. Ron can comfort him. "I don't know why I feel this way," he tells his wife when he gets home. "I guess I just haven't gotten over waiting all that time for him."

But Mort's not a guy to let time go by without contact. A few weeks later he calls in a panic. It's evening and Jerry is depressed. He has just been told that he'll probably lose his job at the end of the month.

"Hey, Jer, it's Mort."

"Oh, hi," Jerry says, obviously depressed.

Mort doesn't pick up on the tone in Jerry's voice at all.

"You'll never guess what happened," Mort huffs through the phone. "Right in the middle of an argument, Mona took all her stuff and left."

Jerry is shocked into attention. The depression in his voice, which Mort never heard, is replaced by concern.

"God, Mort, that's terrible. Right out of the blue?"

"I can't really even talk about it. It's so crazy."

"I'll get right over there," Jerry says instinctively.

"Oh, no. I'm kinda out of it. Drank nearly a bottle of vodka. Funny. I wanted to talk but now I don't think I can. Maybe I'll take a ride to the beach or something."

"Hey, Mort. You can't handle that kind of liquor. Don't go anywhere. I'll come right over."

As soon as Jerry hangs up the phone, it rings. It's Ron. "Did ya hear about Mort?"

"Yeah, I was just about to jump on over there."

"Me, too. Maybe we'll be able to figure out something to do between the two of us."

"Tonight you'll probably be the only one able to figure out anything. I'm so down, I could easily match Mort's depression."

"What's happening?"

"I just found out I'm gonna lose my job. The company's phasing out—"

"We'd better get over to Mort's quickly," Ron interrupts. How's about telling me about your job on the way?"

"Oh, yeah, sure," Jerry says resignedly. "Drop by here and pick me up, OK?"

The two drive over to Mort's in relative silence, both worried about Mort's condition. When they get to his house they find him staring at the TV. Jerry goes into the kitchen to make coffee. Alone, he starts to think about himself, his job, his future. He starts to panic. The whole day floods in on him and he can't think straight.

"Ron," he says, coming out of the kitchen with the coffee. "I'm really panicked about my job. I don't know what the hell I'm gonna do."

Ron and Mort look up from the couch, puzzled. Neither responds.

"Here, Mort," Jerry offers the coffee. "You like it with two sugars, don't you?"

Now Ron's irritated. "Jerry, maybe this isn't the time to be talking about your job. I mean, that's not going to happen for another month and we've got some real problems here right now."

"Oh, no, Ron," Mort answers. "Jerry's got to think about what he's going to do about work. That's really important. The fact that Mona left me is something that's already happened. Nothing much I can do about that now. Nothing. I don't think I'll ever be able to patch things up with her. I'm such a mess. You don't really know what it's like to have your woman split on you until it actually happens."

"Don't you think there's a chance of you two getting back together?" Jerry asks, returning the conversation to Mort.

"I don't know. I just don't know."

"Well, you haven't had much time to think," Ron says to comfort Mort. "We'll figure something out."

Ron and Jerry leave Mort asleep. In the car on the way home they talk about Mort and Mona, about Mort's lawsuit. Neither mentions Jerry's job.

It's a couple of weeks later and Jerry has been sending applications everywhere and calling connections to see about work. He calls Mort, hoping Mort knows someone who knows someone.

"Hi, Mort. How have you been?"

"Not bad. Doing better than I thought, thanks to you and Ron. How about yourself?"

"To tell you the truth, I'm really in bad shape. Can't figure my way out of this job thing. Don't know what I'm gonna do."

"Jerry, if there's one thing I know about you, it's that you have the ability to find your way out of anything."

"Not this time, Mort. I'm up against the wall."

"Oh, c'mon. You'll find your way out. That's something I've always admired about you. Now, a guy like me—well, I can't even figure out how to squeeze through a new angle Mona's thrown at me. . . ."

The Lummox

The Lummox controls the behavior and expectations of others by being so clumsy and destructive that people expect less of him and eventually avoid giving him any responsibility whatsoever. The Lummox sets these limits without confronting or disclosing his intentions. Among the most active of the Violent Sheep, the Lummox consistently offers "to help."

The help that he offers is a cover for aggression. Invariably he will destroy his target's favorite things "by accident." A Lummox helps wash the dishes and breaks a couple of them, returns a friend's rented car as a favor and dents the door, offers to help type a report and loses a page or spills coffee on it.

His "innocent" passive violence provokes inexpressible violence in his targets—inexpressible because all the Lummox was trying to do was help. Both "trying" and "helping" are virtuous acts that usually exempt the Lummox from any blame. As a result long term relationships with a Lummox can be very self-destructive. His target absorbs so much rage and frustration that he can easily become anxious, depressed, or even physically ill. Eventually, because of the Lummox's limited abilities, he is excused from any duties that he might spoil.

The Lummox is at his destructive best when faced by a figure of authority. The more the Lummox claims to be intimidated by this person, the greater the likelihood that destruction is not far away. A Lummox can make a person feel like a bully while he is "accidentally" destroying that person's most prized possessions.

Jason was twenty-five years old but had those qualities of the lost little boy that he used to maneuver himself out of most adult relationships and expectations. Whenever he felt intimidated, which was most of the time, he became awkward. If someone got too close, and demands lurked on the horizon, he would get flustered and clumsy. He would use the confusion or sympathy that followed as a smokescreen behind which he could retreat into childhood freedom. It was a game well played. It prevented him from going far in "the marketplace," a world he wasn't too crazy about anyway, but it also protected him from the expectations of others, and that alone, as he saw it, made him the big winner. His quaking helplessness endeared him to many people, especially to women who found little-boy types attractive.

When Jason started working as a teacher, he found that his little boy act wasn't working on Marianne, the principal. She didn't think his sheepish smile or his role as helpless waif was the least big interesting and, aside from some looks of disgust, paid no attention. When Marianne gave instructions and Jason grew wide-eyed with incomprehension, she became impatient and frowned with disapproval. Jason appeared to be intimidated. He would shake and appear frozen-faced. But nothing worked. Usually Jason's shrinking would make even the biggest person stoop, but Marianne wasn't buying. Her expectations did not change. Jason would perform to standard or else.

"For God's sake, Jason, would you stop whining about what you have to do, *for once,* and do it," she would say to him privately. "I don't want to feel like the big bad bully when I ask you to do something that everyone else is doing. Do you understand that?"

Jason didn't understand. All he knew was that his usual defenses weren't getting him the usual exemptions. This awareness made him even more threatened and confused. He became very clumsy.

Known for his mechanical skills and craftsmanship, Jason always offered help whenever he saw Marianne working with tools or putting something together for the school or the teachers.

He would say, "Here Marianne, let me help you," and, for a while, she did.

It was very subtle at first. For every light bulb changed there would be a scratch on the desk where Jason had stepped from the ladder. Everyone knew that Jason was intimidated by authority, and they knew he was trying to be active and involved. So how could he be blamed for a few minor "accidents?"

As Marianne's expectations of Jason's work became clearer, Jason's clumsiness increased. As they worked together longer, his helpful errors became more pointed and destructive. Over a period of months, almost everything important or precious to Marianne was damaged or broken when Jason offered to "help." And after each incident, with something of hers lying smashed or torn or covered with spilled coffee—and usually with Jason suffering some small injury along the way—Marianne would thank Jason and reassure him. After all, he was only trying to help.

"Gee, I'm sorry about the lamp (picture, manuscript, records, . . .), Marianne. I nearly killed myself, but I got the shelves together."

"Don't worry about it, Jason. Are *you* all right?"

Although Jason's fragility didn't budge Marianne, didn't change her expectations of him, the clumsiness had become an effective weapon. Jason could offer help knowing that Marianne would sooner or later refuse it in self-protection. He confirmed his helplessness while offering help. And he was safe from discovery since he wasn't withholding help and appearing childish but offering it in the true spirit of adult community. For anyone to attack this behavior would be like attacking a guest at your birthday party who arrives with a present you don't like. The thought, after all, is what counts.

When Marianne had some of the teachers over for dinner, Jason and his girl friend were among the guests. As the evening went on, everyone else left. Only Marianne, her husband, Jason, and his girl friend Jan remained. Marianne and Jan went into the kitchen and were putting some dishes away when Jason came in. Marianne was reaching for a kitchen step stool to climb up to a top shelf.

"Here, Marianne, let me help you," Jason offered with his usual sincerity. "Let me put them up there," he continued. "I'm taller."

They had spent part of the evening talking about antique furniture. Jan was a beginning collector and Jason enjoyed making furniture, so it was easy for Marianne to share a few of her special prizes with them. One of them was a set of early American kitchen chairs with cane seats.

One of those cane seats made an awful sound as Jason's foot

went through it. No more than a second could have passed before that awful sound was followed by the crash of dishes.

"Damn! I'm sorry, Marianne. I'm really sorry. I was just trying to get the things up on the shelf when the chair gave way. God, I think I twisted my ankle. Let me help clean up. You have a broom?"

Jason, of course, wasn't fired. But to put an end to the slow destruction of everything around her, Marianne very carefully avoided Jason's offers for help. He was a very clumsy person. But he meant well.

The Conspicuous Non-assumer

The Conspicuous Non-assumer lives at the edge of active violence. Though he doesn't commit harmful acts, he complies with violence by letting it happen. Unlike the Innocent Bystander, whom you'll meet later, the Conspicuous Non-assumer isn't the messenger with the bad news. The Conspicuous Non-assumer is concerned with himself, not the happenings around him.

The embodiment of violent passivity, he can walk past two young children playing with a broken bottle and say, "People really ought to supervise their children," without taking the bottle away from the kids himself. He can ignore the sounds of a forced entry coming from his neighbor's house and say, "One thing people can say about me: I mind my own business." He often rationalizes his actions under a theoretical banner. The Conspicuous Non-assumer is usually a great believer in individual freedom and in other people's personal responsibility. He uses those beliefs to exempt himself from complicity in overt violence.

He is one of the most insidious members of the Flock because his violence involves doing nothing. When he is spotted or uncovered, he often provokes open retaliation and accusations, which he dismisses with some pseudo-philosophical excuse.

CONSPICUOUS NON-ASSUMER I

We're sitting in a restaurant in Los Angeles and look up when we hear the screams of a child, who unfortunately has been seated with his mother and father behind us. The parents are sitting in a curved booth, with the child at the open end "head" of the table in a highchair provided by the management.

"What do you want, Jonathan? There's a lot of good things here," the father says to the three-year-old, who stops screaming only long enough to answer loudly, "I want a hot dog."

"There are no hot dogs, darling," says mother, who proceeds to recite for the kid every item on the very long menu.

The parents are dressed in the unmistakable costume of the

academic liberal: mother in long country dress and spectacles, father in levis with a wool shirt. The child's mode of transportation, a back rack, is resting on the seat next to daddy.

There follows a long propaganda speech for roast turkey. The three-year-old screamer is told about all the bad things in hot dogs and that roast turkey is "really good stuff."

The kid buys none of this and screams full blast, uninterrupted by the mother or father. The waitress, seeing that the parents are going to be no help in turning off the noise, brings the child some crackers. The kid promptly rips open the crackers and throws them onto the carpet.

"Jonathan, now the choice is up to you. Do you want some roast turkey?" mama persists.

Jonathan really can't hear the question over his self-imposed din, and doesn't stop to ask for a rerun.

The waitress brings more crackers. The kid rips them open and crumbles them onto the floor. The waitress is now somewhat irritated and stays close by to take the order as quickly as possible and get this whole thing behind her.

"I want a hot dog. I want a hot dog," screams Jonathan.

The waitress comes over, thinking she has an opening.

"Little boy, we don't have any hot dogs. But we have hamburgers. Would you like—"

"Excuse me," says the man in the logger costume, "this is our child and we want him to be able to make up his own mind. It's very important for him to make his own choice and I'd appreciate it if you'd just give him a chance. He is a person, you know."

More screaming. The waitress retreats to the coffee urn. About a hundred people in this restaurant are being assaulted by one child's screaming and carrying on.

Comments from the surrounding tables, some where young children are sitting quietly eating, meet with glaring defiance from both mother and father, who apparently see this struggle with the surrounding diners as a war of principle. Finally, after fifteen minutes more of mock decision-making, the mother summons the waitress.

"He wants the roast turkey," she says unashamedly, and then proceeds to give her and her husband's order. The kid doesn't seem to agree with the decision he has made. He throws the salt shaker on the floor.

The waitress brings the order with record speed. The kid takes a bite of the roast turkey and throws the rest on the floor. Waitress and busboys are becoming openly irritated and the surrounding diners openly aggressive. The parents pay no attention to this but suddenly begin to berate the waitress, finally asking to see the manager. The kid is now screaming nonstop.

To the requests from the people around her that she do something with her child so that they can finish their dinners in peace the mother responds: "You have your ways of raising your children and we have ours." Her attention is immediately somewhere else.

The manager comes, patiently listens to the complaints about this rotten waitress who doesn't understand children and freedom, and allows the family to have their say, pay their check, and leave. They leave no tip. They've been insulted.

As the family leaves, to sighs of relief and some applause, the father turns to no one in particular and, in a voice loud enough for all to hear, says: "This place has the worst service in the world!"

CONSPICUOUS NON-ASSUMER II

It was a rooster.

He was sure it was a rooster. But it was only four o'clock in the morning and it was still pitch black outside, no sunrise for more than an hour yet.

"A rooster with a screwed-up timer," he thought to himself, "and here, in the middle of the city."

Everybody knows that anything can happen in the middle of a city, but he was surprised nonetheless that this particular thing had happened just an hour after he had dropped off to sleep. Even worse, it didn't seem about to stop.

He propped himself up on his elbows and shook out some of the sleep still lodged between his ears. Maybe he imagined it. Maybe he was having a rooster dream. Maybe . . .

"Coo-oo-oo-ooooooooh." It came tearing through the night like a scream for help. "Co-oo-oo-oooooh!" It was a rooster for sure, the real thing. And he wished it were dead.

Forget the farm fantasies, the little-house-on-the-prairie romanticism, the healthy retreat to country life. This was Wednesday morning, and he had a big meeting in less time than it would take him to catch up on the remnants of a night's sleep. The rooster might just as well have been a fire engine or a small nuclear weapon. He was awake and he hated it.

For the next two nights the rooster repeated its performance. He had to do something about that rooster or else sleep in daylight. It wasn't difficult to tell where the noise came from. The direction of the hateful sounds was easy to fix in the dead of night. The rooster was living next door, in the yard of a man who gave counsel to the young and willing. A guru.

So he prepared to meet the guru. He had seen him on a few occasions but never met him. There was an ordinariness about the guru that could have fooled anyone into thinking that he was a regular person. But then the requirements for gurus these days are not what they used to be.

He straightened himself up, tucked his shirt in his pants, and walked next door to ask the guru the meaning of quiet and to enlist his help in achieving peace and tranquillity, here and now, in the bed he slept in only a few feet from the guru's back yard and the parading rooster. It was an unusual experience. How many people visit a guru in the middle of a city to ask his help in silencing a rooster?

A frail man came to the door looking just like anyone else, only there was a little less of him.

"Hello." Neighborly tone. "I'm your neighbor next door. I wonder if we could talk for a minute?"

The guru nodded and said, "Yes," with a distant gaze that could come only from knowing truth or sniffing glue.

He began to tell the guru the story about the rooster and how it was keeping him from sleeping and how that was very bad karma. The guru listened. Then he asked an imponderable question.

"What makes you think that this is my chicken?" he said, in staccato tones that would have let anyone know that he was either a guru or a robot.

"No, it's not a chicken. It's a rooster. And I didn't know that it wasn't yours. But I do know that the noise it's making is coming from your back yard, right under my bedroom window."

The guru persisted: "I don't own a chicken."

"Then would you mind if I went into your yard and took the visiting rooster and gave him to one of our local barnyard zoos?"

"It is not my chicken. So I cannot give him to you," said the guru, at least acknowledging the chicken's gender.

"Look," he said, "I don't want to get into a whole elaborate discussion about ownership and your right to make these kinds of decisions. What I would like is to relocate the rooster so that I can sleep. We are neighbors, you know, and, really, it would be a very neighborly thing to do if you would just let me sleep."

"If you have trouble sleeping, that is your sickness," said the guru, as if this whole visit was a cover for some seat-of-the-pants spiritual counseling.

"If it is sickness for me to want to sleep, I suppose I am very sick, since I come down with the urge to do it nearly every night. And I am getting very irritated at your indifference to my problem," he said, beginning to feel the veins in his neck stand out.

The wispy guru looked him in the eye and repeated his chant. "It is not my chicken. The chicken came in one day and chose to live here. It is not my chicken and it is not up to me to move it."

"Then I guess it's up to me," the visitor said, moving toward the back yard. "I don't want to cause you any spiritual conflicts. I'll take care of relocating the rooster myself."

"No," said the guru. "It gives great pleasure to my children and to the people who come here."

"That's very nice for them," he said, "but this is, after all, the middle of the city and not a communal farm. I can appreciate your wanting to have your own amusement park, but I had hoped you would appreciate the trouble it is causing me."

"You are bringing disharmony," the guru accused.

"I'll have that goddamn chicken for dinner," the neighbor yelled.

"You are angry and I do not believe that we can discuss this any longer."

"I'm gonna take *you* to Colonel Sanders." He knew he had already lost the war.

"Have you considered curing yourself?" the guru added.

"I'll show you how I'll cure myself, you sonofabitch." The visitor lifted the little man off the ground with one hand. He startled himself. The guru was looking somewhat less distant. Realizing what he had done, the petitioner put the little man down, backed away, and went home.

He didn't sleep much for the next two weeks. Starting at four A.M. the rooster crowed nonstop. He took no time off for weekends or terrible hangovers. But he was, after all, alone, and roosters are not known to be at peace without the occasional company of the female of their kind.

Finally, the Humane Society came. The guru told them, "It's not my chicken," but refused to let them come in and remove it. So, after giving the guru a citation for creating a nuisance and owning (whether he admitted it or not) a barnyard animal in a residential area, the long arm of the law at last offered a perch for a dispossessed rooster.

He saw the guru again shortly after the Humane Society took away the rooster. The guru and his guruees were continuing their practice of harmony with the universe (bounded by the precise property lines around the guru's house). Van loads of truth seekers, their yins and yangs drying in the California sun, were digging a slit trench to process their organic garbage. It was right under their neighbor's bedroom window, in the area the rooster had vacated. The trench was the group's newest move toward spiritual harmony through participation in the recycling of matter. One could see and smell the fermenting garbage as it moved through its stages of earthly visibility, decay, and return to the energy of the universe. One could see the flies and other small insects and animals that helped the garbage on its way.

One could see and smell everything from the neighbor's bedroom window.

The Connection

The Connection gets his name from the illicit narcotics trade. The drug dealer, the "pusher" or the "connection," creates, encourages, and feeds the dependency of his customers, then demonstrates his control by periodically making his addicts sweat for the goods.

The Connection, as he exists in the Flock, usually ties himself to his targets by the good he can do their career. He is the link to power and has real or ascribed expertise, a valued opinion, or personal decision-making power that is accepted as a requisite to someone else's success. The Connection expresses his violence passively by withholding his expertise, approval, or permission and disregarding the resulting frustration, confusion, and suffering.

A master of the mixed or double message, attracting and holding people with praise or promises while denying them their elevated hopes or dreams, the Connection abuses his power. He rationalizes his acts of omission, disorganization, or misunderstanding by saying that he is overburdened and oppressed by his position and the demanding mob of people (they who have taken his bait) dependent upon him. The Connection makes himself appear the victim of his own success.

The Connection both pushes dreams and claims to be able to realize them. Thus he can both motivate and frustrate. He may be the lawyer who tells you that you "can't lose" and then, after getting your case (and money), fails to keep in touch with you. When he is finally available, he admits that your case is more complicated than it originally seemed and will take years in the courts. He may advise you to settle out of court, in a complete turnabout from his original statement that this was a case that "couldn't lose."

He may be a recording agent who says you have "star potential," then, once he signs you to a contract, is too busy with his established clients to connect you with any record companies.

He may be a film producer, an art gallery owner, or invention marketeer, who, after you have been encouraged and "hooked" into dependency, is unavailable to do whatever he originally promised.

The difference between the Connection and constructive "gatekeepers" lies in the discrepancy between what each promises and what each actually delivers. The Connection keeps his targets in exclusive, prolonged, and destructive dependency.

The only difference between the Connection and the con man is one of intent. The con man intends to swindle his targets, while the Connection swindles them unintentionally.

"Jim, call Phil Cavel in Boston. Julie."

The telegram came from the publicity director of Jim's publisher and included the number he was to call. Phil Cavel was the head of the Boston Speaker's Bureau, one of the world's largest booking agencies for the lecture circuit of colleges, conferences, and conventions. Jim was anxious to return the call, since it might mean a leap from what was now an occasional invitation to a regular speaking schedule. Authors and others who caught the public fancy were well paid for their appearances, and Jim was excited about the rewards. But getting in the circuit was another thing—like an exclusive club. Now he might get a shot at it.

The phone seemed to ring for minutes before a woman's voice said, "Boston Speaker's Bureau."

"I'm returning Phil Cavel's call," said Jim, identifying himself, his publisher, and his latest book.

With one click of the phone Phil Cavel himself was on the other end, offering a warm reception and hyperbolic praise of Jim's work.

"We've got to have you on our fall list," Phil said, getting directly to the point. "You're unique. Your books are marvelous and college audiences will love you. How about coming up to Boston and working out the details? I know we can get you all the bookings you can handle and start off at fifteen hundred a throw, but let's get together and talk about it. When can you come?"

"I don't know," said Jim, overwhelmed. "How about sometime next week?"

In the middle of the following week, Jim flew to Boston to meet Phil Cavel in person. The meeting was like a reunion of old friends. Cavel introduced Jim to all the members of the Bureau staff and made a point of telling them, "Jim's going to be with us for the fall list," even before details had been discussed or contracts signed.

The courtship continued at lunch and back in Phil Cavel's office, where he boasted, "There are other lecture bureaus, but none of them have the clout we have."

Contracts appeared and were studied and signed. Everything in them seemed to confirm Phil's promises. Jim flew back home to work and to wait for the call that would mean the first swing on the circuit.

After several weeks had passed with no word from Phil, Jim found that he couldn't concentrate on his work. He didn't know whether to launch into either of his two long writing projects, because he wasn't certain how much time he would have before he would be interrupted to speak. He called Cavel.

"I'm really sorry I didn't get back to you," was Phil's ready response. "I've lost a secretary and everything around here is backed up as a result. I'm taking your presentation to the committee this week and then we should have things on the road."

"Committee? What committee?" Jim was surprised.

"Oh, well, everything around here is done by committee. All the account people get together and decide how to proceed with each of our clients. That way everyone knows what everyone else is doing and we can get optimum effectiveness and efficiency in our college contacts. It prevents conflicting scheduling. That kind of thing."

"Okay," said Jim. "When will I hear from you?"

"Oh, by the end of next week."

Two weeks passed with no call from Cavel.

In the meantime Jim got a call from a university asking him to speak at a conference. Knowing that his contract with the Bureau gave them "exclusive" rights to book his appearances, Jim called Cavel to find out how to handle the invitation and to ask what was going on.

Cavel's new secretary said he was in a meeting, took Jim's message, and said Cavel would call back the next day.

When Cavel didn't call the next day, Jim called Boston again, and this time Cavel answered himself.

"Hi, Jim. I was just going to call you. We're having a hard time with the schedule. The colleges aren't getting back to us and we're running way behind. You can't believe the craziness around here. Don't worry, though. As soon as we get some firm commitment, I'll call you."

"What about the invitation I got directly? How should I handle that?" Jim asked with some annoyance.

"Just set it up any way you want. It's great that they called you. It'll help get the committee moving. Let me know how it goes. In any case, I'll call you a week from today. We should have your itinerary by then."

By now Jim was anxious. It was almost impossible to concentrate. While he was waiting for Cavel to call his work routine was falling apart.

Finally, after the promised call didn't come, Jim called Boston again. This time he was in a rage. Between the flight to Boston and all the phone calls, Cavel's "expertise" had already cost him more than five hundred dollars and the only speaking dates he had were made on his own.

After asking who was calling, Cavel's secretary said he wasn't in but that she would leave the message.

A few days later Cavel called.

"Jim, I'm sorry." Cavel sounded depressed. "I just can't get the committee enthused. I'm doing what I can, but you know, my hands are tied. Between the colleges, the committee, and our established clients, it's really a crazy game here."

After all the buildup and grand plans, Jim felt defeated and deflated. Compared to the dream he had bought, his original accomplishments and success seemed smaller, almost insignificant.

"I sure thought things would work out differently," Cavel muttered in Jim's silence. "But you never can tell what the public wants."

Jim was still at a loss for words.

"Well," Cavel sighed, "I'll keep in touch."

Babes

Babes are seductively helpless. So many things frighten or intimidate them that they often don't even have to ask for help. Simply by expressing their fears or feelings of ineptitude they make people want to rescue them.

Once help is offered to Babe it is not very easy to withdraw. What may start out as a neighborly offer to help change a tire ("Mechanical things just freak me out," says Babe) can lead to every automotive and household repair that Babe finds "frightening," "depressing," or "impossible."

Babes can't quite cope. They can't quite understand. So they get others to cope and understand for them. They succeed partly by their skill in making people who might otherwise feel unappreciated or even incapable feel inordinately appreciated and capable. "I've never met anyone who 1) is so good with their hands, 2) is such a good person, 3) knows so much about these things, etc." Babe is difficult to resist and even more difficult to abandon.

The demands of Babes escalate. Most Babes will try to keep their victims in a kind of permanent servitude. Some will go over the line and demand more than the helper is willing to give. When that happens and the helper's gratification ebbs into resentment at being had, the helper, who has become the dupe, turns Babe down. The "terrific goodness" of the helper is then erased from Babe's awareness, along with any sense of obligation or responsibility.

Babe's passive violence comes out of what psychologist Fritz Redl calls "absurdity of demand" and the effect of the ruse of helplessness on the helper.

Once almost exclusively a woman's role, Babe has become a popular pose with men. ("I just can't figure out how these vacuum cleaner things are supposed to work." "Which button do you push to start the dishwasher, anyway?")

Babes are most often found within the victim's family, in close relationships, among neighbors, or in the office.

* * *

Paul had some reservations about having a neighbor downstairs. He wanted to rent a house and have it all to himself. But when he saw the view and heard the price of this house, he decided he would make a concession and give up a little privacy. Besides, he thought, the man who lived in the converted basement apartment was old and dignified and seemed to mind his own business.

The first few weeks in his new home flew by without incident. Mr. Mondello, Paul's downstairs neighbor, had invited him in for a glass of sherry and Paul had reciprocated with an invitation to have coffee. Mondello didn't complain about Paul's housewarming party or when he played his stereo rather loudly. His proximity didn't affect the way Paul wanted to live.

One day when Paul arrived home, he saw Mondello standing in front of a car parked in the driveway. Its hood was up.

"Something the matter?" Paul asked casually.

"I don't know anything about these machines." Mondello's voice was shaking. "It just doesn't seem to want to go."

"Let me take a look," Paul offered, though he wasn't much of a mechanic himself. He studied the smoking engine. Then he noticed something. The fan belt was lying on the ground under the car. Because the fan wasn't turning, the car was overheating. Even Paul could tell that.

"What you need, Mr. Mondello, is a new fan belt. I think that's your problem."

"I'm so lucky," said Mondello, "to live downstairs from a real mechanic. You know what it would have cost me to get the car towed into a station to have someone look at it? And they never would have told me the truth, besides. Here you come along and just take a look at it and you know right away what's the matter.

"Tell me," Mondello continued, "will it be very much of an imposition for you to get a fan belt and put it on the car? I wouldn't ask if I didn't have an important appointment with my doctor."

"I'll tell you what," Paul replied. "I'll drive down to the gas station with you and we'll pick up a fan belt, come back, and put it on in no time."

"I don't believe my luck," said Mondello. "First you help me find the problem with the car and then you offer to fix it. I'm a very lucky man to have a neighbor like you."

"Aw, forget it," Paul said as he picked up the fan belt and moved towards his own car, with Mr. Mondello not far behind.

They found a service station and bought the new fan belt. On the way back home, Mondello was glowing with appreciation for this "very unusual, unselfish thing you are doing."

Paul struggled with the fan belt and finally succeeded in getting it on over the fan and engine pulleys. He was greasy, tired, and an hour behind schedule, but he felt good about it. Mondello was off to the doctor.

A few days passed before Mr. Mondello called Paul to tell him that he thought he smelled gas leaking. Paul went downstairs to see whether there was any danger and didn't smell anything.

"It scares me sometimes to think about what could happen to me, all alone here, if something serious happened," Mondello said.

"Don't worry," said Paul. "I'm just upstairs, so there's nothing to worry about."

Mondello shook his head and looked at Paul wistfully. "You don't know what a comfort it is to have you here," he said.

"Forget it," Paul responded reflexively. But the words felt good. He'd never felt much of a help to anyone. And Mondello offered so many opportunities for him to be helpful.

One night about four A.M., Paul awoke to loud banging. At first he thought that someone was trying to break into his house, and then he found that the banging was coming from his floor— Mondello's ceiling. Throwing on his clothes, he ran downstairs. After knocking and getting no response Paul tried Mondello's door. It was unlocked. Paul slowly stepped into the basement apartment. Mondello was sitting in bed banging on his ceiling with a long stick.

"What's the matter?" Paul asked. "Why are you doing that?"

"I think I'm having a problem with my diabetes," Mondello said as he began shaking. "I need to call the doctor."

"How about if I call an ambulance?" Paul asked, frightened that Mondello could be in serious trouble.

"I'm really afraid of those ambulance people." Mondello was now crying. "You know how they are. They take their time getting here and then they take your money and, well, I just don't know what to do."

"I'm going to call the hospital for an ambulance," said Paul, still wiping the sleep from his eyes.

"God bless you," said Mondello. "But I'm so afraid of those people. They've been here before. It was horrible. Could you . . . I mean it's more than I should ask, but could *you* take me?"

Paul thought for a minute and then said, "Sure, come on, I'll help you get dressed."

Paul drove him to the hospital. By the time Mondello was treated, it was almost time for Paul to get up and go to work.

"I'll never forget you for this," said Mondello on the way home. "There aren't good Christian people like you around anymore. Anyone else would have just turned over and gone back to sleep. You're a very special person."

Over the next several weeks Paul was called downstairs to fix a telephone, so that Mondello wouldn't be out of touch with the hospital, help find a missing pair of glasses "just in case I have to call the doctor or drive somewhere," and "help" carry out Mondello's garbage, which, it turned out, was extraordinarily heavy.

On one garbage day, Paul ventured a look into Mondello's trash can to see what was so damned heavy. It was filled with liquor bottles. Mondello's diabetic attacks were self-inflicted, the result of heavy drinking.

"Jesus," said Paul, "I've been a damned jerk. I've been playing nursemaid to an alcoholic. Jesus. A diabetic alcoholic."

The next time Mondello needed Paul's special expertise, Paul refused.

"I'm sorry, Mr. Mondello," he said, "but if you need someone to take care of you, I suggest you hire a handyman or a companion. I've got problems of my own, and you're frankly getting to be a real pain."

Mondello studied Paul's face carefully. "You're just like every other selfish sonofabitch." He seemed stronger than ever. "I should have known better than to trust you."

Soon after, Paul moved into a place with no view and higher rent. His experience with Mondello left him angry and bitter. It took him a long time to forget the Mondello matter.

Mondello is still in his basement apartment. He is most helpless when there is a tenant upstairs.

The Systems Tangler

If the Systems Tangler had a motto, it would be, "For every system there is a monkey wrench." His passively violent response to authority is to undermine every system he encounters, from political club or bridge club to office and school. In the process people get hurt.

The Systems Tangler doesn't attack people but systems. He is always the outsider, the rebel whose only cause is to right the inequities he sees in a system. His object is to disrupt and his motive is to feel a *transient* surge of power and authority. He may lead walkouts, strikes, protests, and other forms of opposition, but he never sustains leadership or directs the people who have followed him. He is not interested in constructing a "good" system.

The Systems Tangler is addicted to destruction. He uses philosophical pretexts to manipulate and confuse. Once his righteous indignation is in jeopardy of being seen as a cover for his real motive, to destroy, he moves on to more fertile ground. Political groups, religious cults, and social movements are especially attractive to the Systems Tangler, who gains access to these groups with suggestions for running them more smoothly.

While the strategies of the Systems Tangler may appear to be more overt than the usual passive tactics of the Flock, his goals and motives are covert and deceptive. When confronted, the Systems Tangler does not "stand and fight," as his well-constructed image would lead one to expect. He subverts the system behind his ideological cover.

Behind the angry mask of the Systems Tangler is a reservoir of passive violence looking for a target.

Andrea joined the Neighborhood Action Center as an Outreach worker. Her job was to make the Center's services known to community people who might need them. This was a low-income, multi-ethnic neighborhood whose families tended to be

60

conservative and reticent. They stayed mostly to themselves and within their own ethnic groups and distrusted "authority." It was a sensitive job to act as liaison between such a complex community and a social service center, but Andrea had convinced Barbara, the director, that she had both the insight and the stamina to carry it off.

Barbara knew that the Outreach program would take a lot of time and patience. Relationships had to be developed and the very elusive element of trust established. But she was willing to wait.

After only a month, with unspectacular results, Andrea was disappointed and depressed.

"Things just aren't going well," she said to Barbara one day. "I just can't seem to get through to the women. I'm very much involved with women's issues and it's really painful to see how these women are locked into their situations."

"That may be," Barbara counseled her, "but it's not a good idea to go in with a cause. Especially not in this neighborhood, where everybody is so suspicious of outsiders. I think you'd do much better if you put your personal judgments aside and concentrated on getting to know the people as they are."

"I can't compromise my beliefs," Andrea countered. "You're not asking me to overlook how oppressed the women are? Are you?"

"I'm not asking anything of the kind," Barbara answered flatly. "What I am suggesting is that you put down your banner long enough so that people have a chance to get to know you and you them. I think you're building unnecessary barriers instead of bridges."

Andrea went back to the community, and, except for regular meetings, Barbara didn't see Andrea again for another month. When Barbara did it was at her own insistence. People from the neighborhood were calling. Young people were dropping by to speak with Barbara. Andrea was creating a storm of controversy. She had decided that the best way to reach the mothers of the community was to set up a "consciousness-raising group," and she had started with the Puerto Rican mothers because she felt that they were the most oppressed by *machismo*. The neighborhood was buzzing about the Center's being the source of the trouble. Barbara and Andrea met again, alone.

"I asked you to go in slowly, Andrea. I asked you to keep your personal biases out of your first connections with the people here. I can't believe that you would be so heavy-handed as to march into this neighborhood with an issue that is so culturally difficult and expect anything but the angry response you've gotten."

"I expected that kind of response," said Andrea, as if she were at a public forum talking to Norman Mailer. "Change always makes people uncomfortable. But there's no doubt in my mind that it's necessary. And of all places, this is the most oppressive to women that I've ever seen."

"I sympathize with your feelings, Andrea," Barbara answered, "but your feelings are not what you're here to deal with. We have problems of disease and nutrition, housing and police. We have a gigantic drug problem. We need a child care center. There are some real crises here, and while I'm sure we can both indulge ourselves about these problems having roots in the oppression of women, I'm afraid I'm going to have to insist that you keep your organizing along those lines out of your work assignment here."

"Are you telling me that I can't get women together to talk out common problems?" Andrea said, recoiling.

"I'm telling you that your job is to provide a means of getting basic services to people who need them. You are not hired to do your own personal missionary work. Our job is to provide people with some means of survival without making judgments about their style of living or trying to make society over in our image." Barbara was beginning to feel the pressure that Andrea was putting on her. She, a woman, was being forced to order an end to Andrea's feminist organizing.

"Then you're telling me I have to stop my groups."

"You don't have any groups, Andrea. No one is responding to your methods. They're afraid of you. And you're doing damage to the rest of the Center's programs. I'm telling you that you're going to do your job as we originally agreed."

"Or what?" asked Andrea, pushing on.

"Or you're fired," Barbara responded.

* * *

The next day the Center was buzzing. All the women employees were standing in little groups and talking. Some of them came into Barbara's office.

"Is it true you fired Andrea?" they asked.

"No, it's not true. I did tell her that I thought she was pushing her personal issue onto this community and that I didn't think that was fair or reasonable. I gave her the choice of working within these rules or being fired."

"Then she's not fired?"

"Not unless she decides to make her own rules."

"Well, we've never gotten to know Andrea. She's very much to herself and we've never had a chance to see her outside work. But we do know you and we just couldn't believe the things she's saying."

"Like what?" asked Barbara, now catching on that Andrea had spent a very active twenty-four hours.

"Like that you fired her because she's a . . . she's a . . ."

"A what?" asked Barbara.

"A lesbian."

The next day Barbara was visited by members of the Mayor's Commission on Human Rights.

"We have a complaint that you've fired a gay worker. Is that right?" asked the visitors.

"No, it isn't," answered Barbara, and proceeded to tell them exactly what had happened. "As far as I'm concerned," she concluded, "she wasn't fired at all. And I don't know or care about her sexual preferences. Our disagreement had nothing to do with that. It was purely about agency policy and acceptable methods of agency intervention."

"We believe that. But we do have a complaint and we have to answer it. Would you mind filling out these forms? Then we can see if the issue has to go to hearing or not."

Two members of the Center's board of directors called the next day. Someone had phoned and told them that there was going to be a huge demonstration against Barbara at the Center and had wanted to know whether they were aware of her abuses of authority. They also had intimated that Barbara was being less than honest in the use of agency funds.

Barbara was furious but managed to carry on as usual, meeting with kids and families and working out kinks in the bureaucratic maze. She even managed to squeeze in some time during lunch to fill in the forms from the Human Rights Commission.

When Barbara pulled up in front of the Center the next morning, she was surprised to find a large crowd carrying placards and some television cameras and police. She got out of her car and was immediately booed by the twenty or thirty protestors. She didn't know any of them except Andrea, who was smiling victoriously and talking to the television reporters.

"There's a lot going on here that people don't know about," she said ominously to the cameras.

"Exactly what do you mean?" asked a reporter.

"I think it would be better if you asked her," Andrea said, pointing to Barbara, who was walking towards the front door of the Center.

Some of Barbara's workers met her outside.

"Who are these people?" Barbara asked.

"They're from a local civil liberties group," said one woman. "Apparently Andrea has told everyone that you're discriminating against her. I just got a call from a friend at a feminist magazine, and she said that Andrea had called there trying to get them to expose 'successful women who are enemies of equal rights.'"

"Jesus," said Barbara. "What next?"

She fielded questions from reporters, then excused herself to get to her work. The more questions she answered, the more defensive she seemed. It dawned on her that she could not win, that no matter what she said the issues were so tangled they couldn't be separated.

By now the seriousness of Andrea's activities was apparent. The entire future of the Center and Barbara's effectiveness in it were being questioned. Barbara called a staff meeting, then called the members of the board and the Human Rights Commission. She also placed a call to the civil liberties organization sponsoring the picketing.

Finally, all that completed, she called Andrea and asked to meet with her the next morning.

When Andrea arrived, Barbara had gathered everyone whom she knew Andrea had called to spread her slander: the staff, mothers Andrea had tried to organize, people from the city, the board, and the press.

"I've called this meeting just to clear up some issues," Barbara said to Andrea. "First of all, everyone here has been filled in about what really happened here. I don't think there was any misunderstanding between us, and the issues you created were not the issues that separated us. I think what you did was dishonest and destructive. I have no hesitation in firing you for any of that."

Andrea protested, "I don't have to sit here and listen to that. Especially not from you." She got up to leave but the pressure of the group, its obvious disapproval of her retreat, was enough to keep her from leaving.

Barbara continued. "But you brought up an issue in our last meeting. That was an issue of women's rights. You want to organize women's groups in this neighborhood. Despite how I feel about you and what you've done, I think you should have whatever support you need to do that, as long as it is no longer confused with our Outreach program."

Andrea was pale and totally disoriented. She was trying to look confident, but was shaken at the turn of events she hadn't anticipated. Her resistance was gone.

"I've talked to the Human Rights Commission and to the civil liberties people and to our board, and have gotten agreements to support your work for the next month, with meeting space and the use of the office and telephones. That should give you enough resources to get your group together and to find some support of your own," Barbara concluded.

There were a few minutes of total silence.

Then Andrea responded. "Yeah, well . . . that's a good . . . well, I'd like to think about that and. . . ." She began to recover. "But I don't think people should be fooled by you and your program here."

"Well, maybe not," said Barbara, "maybe not. I think people

are going to have to make up their own minds about me. And,"
she added, "about you."

Andrea was seen in the neighborhood twice during the next
month. One of those times she tried unsuccessfully to organize
the women in the Center to strike. The other time she was seen
walking hurriedly down the street and out of sight.

The Victim

The Victim is always in a contest for the place at the bottom. Like the Crisis Monger, the Victim has no capacity to give because he is always preoccupied. But unlike the Crisis Monger, the Victim is not plagued by dramatic or gigantic problems. Instead, he appears to be oppressed by the targets of his own passive violence. This is the unique ability of the Victim: to control his target while keeping up the illusion of his own victimization. In this way, the Victim is able to escape from expected responsibilities.

Since the entire strategy of the Victim is to avoid responsibility, he is most often encountered in families or businesses, where commitments and responsibilities are clearly defined. The Victim mother and father present such an image of being oppressed by their children that they are able to deny responsibilities normally expected of parents. The Victim employee is able to present such an illusion of oppression to his employer that the specific responsibilities for which he was hired are often reduced.

The passive violence of the Victim makes his targets assume his responsibilities while the Victim blames them for forcing him to assume too much. The duties or responsibilities are transferred to the people who are supposed to benefit from them. In a well executed role reversal, the Victim has the target taking over his responsibilities while he retains the publicly observable burden. Amid the resulting confusion and rage, the Victim absorbs enough resentment or oppression to carry his charade further with the same targets or with other people.

The less the Victim actually performs and the more he is able to provoke, the more easily he is able to deny responsibility for anything. No one can beat a Victim, because when he loses, he wins.

VICTIM I

Meg and Len Carrol needed the bathroom and bedroom upstairs painted, and Mr. Shank came highly recommended. The painter was a friend of the Carrols' next door neighbor, and they hired him on his terms, which were unusual: he would work by the hour rather than by the job. The Carrols picked the colors and the paint carefully to coordinate with the new bathroom tiles and the furniture in the bedroom. They bought the most expensive paint and had it waiting on Monday morning when Mr. Shank started work.

Meg and Len looked at Mr. Shank's progress at the end of each day and after four days were surprised to find that the painting hadn't started yet; the preparation wasn't even quite completed. They asked Mr. Shank about this and he had a ready answer.

"I work in the good old-fashioned way," he said in his old country accent. "I don't hurry. It's easy to just go in and throw paint over the walls, but, if you want a really good job, you've got to do it slowly and methodically. People don't do this kind of preparation anymore."

The Carrols looked at each other and smiled. They were, after all, typically American. Push, push, push. They resigned themselves to an extended disruption, imagining that for their patience they would get a paint job that would rival the Sistine Chapel. The promised quality, they felt, would justify the delay.

Little problems came up, like Mr. Shank's not having sandpaper or a paint scraper or patching plaster, but finally, preparation completed, Mr. Shank began painting. The painting went on for another week and Meg and Len were getting furious. They had gone past the point of no return. Drop cloths and paint cans were everywhere and the walls weren't finished.

"How can two rooms take so long?" they both asked.

"I'll be finished tomorrow," Mr. Shank sighed with obvious artistic indulgence. Meg and Len waited to see the finished product of the old-world artisan.

The job was a disaster. Wherever Meg and Len looked, there were unpainted patches of wall and woodwork, sections painted unevenly, others so poorly prepared that the cracks in the wall showed through the paint. After two weeks of preparation and painting, for a job they had thought would take two days, the Carrols had a sloppy and incomplete result.

But this wasn't a hit-and-run operation of some anonymous painter. After all, Mr. Shank was a friend of their neighbors. So they called Mr. Shank and said they wanted to talk to him. After some delay, he returned to the Carrols and was led up to the rooms he had painted.

"This is really bad," said Len. "There are whole sections that haven't been painted. After all the time you had, I think we have a right to expect something better than this."

"What sections?" Mr. Shank replied. "I don't see any sections."

"Right here, look over here. And here. There's no paint," said Meg.

"Where is there no paint? I see paint everywhere. Show me no paint," Shank responded, now irritated.

"Right here." Len pointed.

"How long is that place you're pointing to?" requested Mr. Shank, now assuming the pose of a defense attorney.

"You mean this one?" asked Len.

"Yes."

"Well, I'd say it was about two inches by four inches."

"And *that's* what you're complaining about? Two inches by four inches?"

"No, that's only one of a lot of places. Can't you see what a bad job this is?" Len was getting steamed up.

"Now look," Shank proceeded without really answering, "there's no point in getting angry at me. This was a hard job. The paint you gave me was no good and the walls should have been primed first. I tried to save you all that time and money and this is what I get? Looking at a two-inch place on the wall where you say it doesn't match up?"

"*I* say. Don't you see what I'm showing you here? This is a lousy job and we want it done right or we're not going to pay you until it is." Len was trying to control what had now become a moderate rage.

"I don't know." Mr. Shank was now talking to himself. "I try to do everything to please people but I should know that it's just impossible. I should know by now that whatever I do, no one's satisfied."

"But Mr. Shank, *you're* the one who messed up our walls. What did *we* do?" Meg asked, appealing to rationality.

"Nothing more than anyone else. There's just no way to please some people."

"Mr. Shank," said Len, now following Meg's lead and controlling himself, "look around. Do you see any problems with the paint job you're looking at?"

Mr. Shank waited a few seconds and then, looking like a beaten dog, shook his head from side to side.

Len had reached his limit. He was now shouting. "Do you see there's no paint on this side of the door and none on this window sill and the walls have blotches everywhere? Do you see that or are you blind?"

"I don't see any blotches. If you wanted me to do the job a certain way, you should have let me know at the beginning."

Meg and Len looked at each other and at Mr. Shank in rage and confusion. They were frustrated and angry. Somehow it had come to seem that they were oppressing and exploiting this man, who was, after all, only a painter.

"That's the way of it," Mr. Shank continued on his way out. "People want more than one can give. You know," he asked of no one in particular, "I worked on those rooms for two whole weeks?"

VICTIM II

"Mom," Shirley calls to her mother as she comes in the house from school, "I'd like to have a few friends overnight sometime next week. Is it okay?"

"You know how much I have to do around here," her mother answers. "How can you ask me to do any more when you don't help me enough as it is?"

"Look," Shirley answers, "I'll help you do whatever needs to be done. Just tell me what you need. You know I'll help. I always help."

"Well, you can start with these floors—"

"Okay. But what about my friends. Can I—"

"Don't even ask me about your friends until you do the work you promised. God knows there's only so much one person can do around here. God knows I try."

"I know you try, but can I just once have something that *I* want?"

"This is what I get for trying to do everything around here. A selfish daughter telling me I don't do enough for her."

"But all I'm asking is—"

"You're always asking something. I mean I'm only human. I need some time for myself, too."

"Well, okay. Let me help you. What can I do?"

"You can start with these floors. . . ."

The mother walks away, still commenting to herself. "Kids nowadays. It's just take, take, take. . . ."

The Innocent Bystander

The Innocent Bystander is often the bearer of bad news, but he never helps to solve the problem he introduces. He drops his cargo and stands by, as his target bends under the unwelcome load, becoming angry, violent, and frustrated. When his target catches on that it was the Innocent Bystander who dropped the bomb, the Innocent Bystander backs off with self-righteous excuses: "If that's how you feel, the next time I won't tell you." The damage the Innocent Bystander does—the tension set off, the fights started (always between others), the anger provoked, the fear aroused—is always done innocently, as a bystander, as a "favor."

INNOCENT BYSTANDER I

Bob and Marcia's New York apartment was going to be vacant while they were traveling, so they let Izzy, a friend who was just going through a messy divorce, stay there. His only responsibility, beyond the normal consideration they expected for their home, was to take care of their cat.

This cat, Red, couldn't eat dry cat food. According to their vet, it increased his chances of getting cystitis, a urological infection dangerous to neutered male cats. They made it especially clear to Izzy that the cat should not have any dry food. "That's too bad," he said, "it's so much easier to leave dry food in a bowl for the cat to nibble on without having to change canned cat food twice a day." But that was the condition and he accepted it. In return for this service, they gave their friend the use of their apartment for six months. Not a bad deal for Izzy, but then he was a friend.

One day, after Bob and Marcia had reached Oregon, they received a message at a friend's house to call Izzy. "Red is very sick. It looks like he might not make it," Izzy announced. They put him in touch with their veterinarian and for the next three days the cat's survival was up in the air. When they spoke to the vet on the second day, he told them that he would have to perform a very delicate operation. Red, it turned out, had cystitis.

It turned out also that Izzy had been feeding the cat dry food.

"God, I forgot," he said when they reminded him of his promise not to feed the cat that food, "but he really seemed to like it much better than the canned food."

"But, Izzy, you knew he wasn't supposed to eat that food."

"I don't know why or how I forgot. You know, I've been going through a few changes of my own here. I forgot, but at least he's OK. I mean, it's not like he died. Look, I won't forget again. Don't be worried all the way out there."

Bob and Marcia weren't happy with Izzy's response, but they were three thousand miles away and weren't in a position to have Red sent to them. Anyhow, Red was OK and Izzy had promised never to feed him that food again, so they weren't going to harp on the subject.

When Bob and Marcia returned to New York there were several overdue bills from the veterinarian waiting for them in the mail. It never occurred to them that Izzy, who had caused the problem by his negligence, wouldn't pay the vet bill. He was using the apartment for nothing in exchange for caring for the cat, and, since he was a lawyer, he could well afford to pay.

Puzzled and curious, they called Izzy at his new apartment to ask about the bill. He was indignant.

"You know, I didn't have to call you about Red in the first place. He's your cat. I could have not noticed that he looked sick and just let him die."

INNOCENT BYSTANDER II

"Hello, Janice. It's me, Eve."

"Oh, hi, Eve. I'm in the back. C'mon in."

"You'll never guess what I just saw outside?"

"What?"

"Some guy broke into your car."

"WHAT?"

"Yeah. He was just loosening the window when I came by."

"Is he still there?"

"I don't know."

"You saw him do it?"

"Yeah, just now before I came in."

"Why the hell didn't you do anything?"

"I DID. I just ran in to tell you."

"No, dummy!" Janice shouts as she runs out towards her car. "Why didn't you stop him?"

"God, Janice, I could have let the whole thing pass. Maybe I should have. Now I'm sorry I said anything. Wow. That's what I get for being a friend."

The Power Swindler

The Power Swindler discredits anyone with power through passively violent tactics that make his target appear capricious or corrupt. He makes a "star" stop a conversation or put aside dinner to acknowledge him by signing an autograph, and, in doing this, he achieves a kind of power of his own. By demanding responses from renowned experts, he convinces himself that he shares their expertise. He can take up the time of an elected official to discuss a small matter. Anyone in power who turns him down or considers him rude or intrusive he immediately and publicly brands a fake, an elitist, an egoist, or a brute.

The Power Swindler believes that anyone in power should "be able to handle it." What he means is that anyone in power should be available to him. The Power Swindler's absurd expectations dehumanize power and make anyone who has it a different kind of being from himself.

The Power Swindler doesn't compete for power. He doesn't want it. What he wants is to exploit power, demean it, and use it for his own ends. By successfully compromising a powerful figure he achieves equality with greatness.

(Herbert Gold is a novelist whose most recent book is *Waiting for Cordelia*. His description of a Power Swindler which follows originally appeared in the *San Francisco Chronicle*.)

A young man called because he was doing an article about publishing first novels in San Francisco. "You mean writing them, don't you?" I asked.

"Oh, yeah. But the problem, bottom line, is how to make the contacts so you can publish it."

"No, Sir. The problem, bottom line, is to make the contact so you can write it. There's only one contact you need to make."

I didn't want to have to tell him what that was. If he was a writer, he should be able to figure it out. Even by telephone I could tell he was thinking, and he turned kind of slow and thoughtful. Maybe he had interrupted my morning. He regretted this, if so. He wanted to gain my favor again.

It was one of those sunny dry mornings in San Francisco, a wisp of fog over the bay, when a fellow considers whether to remember first love or have another cup of coffee. If the metabolism works right, you can do both at the same time. He asked: "Who's a good agent in San Francisco?"

Naturally I was relieved not to have to write my book, but instead I could be informational, helpful, irritated, and patronizing. All this pleases a man, although it leaves a bit of ego hangover. I talked to him about scouts, editors, magazines, small-press publishers. I assured him that one writes by writing, not by acquaintances; and if you're talking about novels, one publishes in the same way, by writing the book.

Knowing people won't even save postage. Perhaps non-fiction is different, and you get a publisher by knowing someone, not by writing a book. But I doubt it.

The young man said he was writing an article. I suggested he was a bruised would-be, searching to squeeze some juice out of the rind of his rejection slips. He needed to know *why*. You see, I am sorry enough for him to create a flowery, sentimental, slightly acid metaphor.

"It's difficult, I agree," I said. "First novels are printed, but many aren't. However, second and third and fifth novels also find trouble getting published, or distributed, or read. The problem is never solved, Sir."

His silence now meant: why do you keep calling me "Sir"?

"Man, I haven't got the answer," I said.

He was encouraged. "Could we get together and rap about writing?"

I smelled cigarettes, coffee, hamburgers, and a slow exhalation of advice from me. The first smells were okay, but not the last. Who knows, I thought, if he were a pretty girl, I would be more indulgent. And so out of shame I said: "Sure, come up and I'll see what I can do for you. But I think I've told you everything."

And that was the sadness of it. All he wanted to know was how-to. I'm not sure I could tell him why, or what, or even show him the way to ask those questions. He was on his way and I was putting on the mask.

He arrived and I thought: Nothing but agony here. He was a thin, harassed, groovy kid, who had smoked a lot of grass (hair, teeth) and used a little cocaine or speed (skinny, spidery) on top of a lot of good California sun and food and middle-class parents (tall, big-boned). He reached out to take my hand. His clean and dry, and the gesture meant to be respectful, I think. It left no fingerprints. I made instant coffee. We looked at the Trans-America building across Russian Hill and North Beach.

"How old are you?" I asked.

He sighed. He put more sugar in and stirred and gazed at me.

We talked about life and love and the difficulty of finding a place in the world and the passion for literature and the dangers of success and failure. We drank more coffee, past the coffee peak, and we talked some more about fate and desperation and responsibility and the youth of America.

"My men's group," he murmured, knowing he would have to confess to them as he now copped out to me. "My men's group thinks I'm still performance-oriented. I'm success-hungry. I can't relax, it's my hangup from my parents. I want to get to the top. 'Why write for others?' they ask me. We have a community right here. I can't answer that, but somehow, talking it all out in my men's group doesn't hack it for me."

"You're an artist and you can't look back," I said.

"Huh?"

"Bob Dylan song," I said.

"The book has two parts. Part One: My Lovers, Female. I call that Part the First. Part Two: My Lovers, Male. It's fictionalized, of course. Part the Second. I change all the names except maybe my own. Fischer-Hoffman therapy helped me work it through, plus I got my group, only they're not so supportive anymore since I had the thing Xeroxed and I'm sending it out. I'd like to sell it as well as finding the truth about myself and my lovers. I paid my dues, man. I want to live a little better. As an old pro, I thought, you could advise."

"Thank you for that compliment."

His eyes burned into mine. We were making contact. He communicated. Communication was not the problem; it was what he communicated that troubled me. Nevertheless, in my own way, I sought to remain in touch.

"You like to visit our group one time?" he asked. "You wouldn't have to tell the truth the first time, just listen. I think you could handle it, man."

You can come free of any charge, he was saying.

He pulled at the ends of his mustache. It was a well-tugged drop-out mustache. He knew that half of an I-Thou relationship involved listening, and so, humming softly, he listened me out. And so, on the third cup of coffee I once more asked this skinny, nervous kid that first question which he had not yet answered: "How old are you?"

"Forty," he said.

The Web Spinner

The Web Spinner invites his victim into webs that are loaded with tangles and sticky obstacles. Like the spider, the Web Spinner creates the traps and then watches as his victim tries to extricate himself.

The Web Spinner is an unusual member of the Flock because he makes overt demands and sets precise limits that always seem, at first, simple and reasonable. The passive violence lies in his ability to make his target feel obligated, confused, and disoriented, as his "simple requests" escalate into numerous complicated expectations.

The Web Spinner hides a Pandora's Box of entangling requirements behind some simple openers. The more anyone gets involved, the more passively inflicted torment lies ahead.

A Web Spinner may have special religious beliefs, dietary or health needs, aversions, allergies, or well-founded fears. He may be sensitive about lateness, protocol, or "swear words." He may request one of many simple concessions. Once he establishes the target's willingness to accommodate, the Web Spinner's "simple requests" become convoluted demands.

"Why don't we meet?" said Eve. She was at Grand Central Station.

Eve and Rita had never met even though they were first cousins. Nearly ten years older than Rita, Eve had left home and gone off to study music and then to Europe, where she had married and settled. Now she was in New York City, just passing through until her morning plane would take her back to Holland.

"I'd love to meet. Are you staying somewhere?" Rita answered, happy and confused at this unexpected connection with someone who had only existed in family stories of growing up.

"No. I'm not. I'd love to see you," Eve replied.

"Well, look, just grab a cab and come straight downtown. We're really easy to find from where you are in midtown; you can

be here within half an hour. We'll have dinner and we can talk."
Rita was beginning to get excited.

"A cab?" said Eve. "I'm afraid I'll get lost. I have a kind of
accent that you may be able to hear and I'm afraid cab drivers will
know I'm a foreigner and take advantage." She laughed, but Rita
could tell she was concerned.

"Well, it is New York," Rita told herself, as if that revelation
had some meaning, "maybe we should go and get her."

So at rush hour on a Friday afternoon Rita and Gary, her
husband, got their car out of its burial place in the parking
lot and inched their way uptown to pick up the expatriate
cousin.

When they finally reached Grand Central, Eve was outside
surrounded by suitcases and cardboard boxes.

Rita got out and did all the hugging and kissing that long-lost
relatives do, and finally got around to getting the truckload of
boxes into the Mustang.

"Why don't you leave your luggage checked in Grand Central
or the midtown airlines terminal?" Rita suggested as she and
Gary tried to find rope to strap the boxes onto the top of the car.
"At least the things you won't need tonight. Then tomorrow
morning you can stop back on your way out and pick them up. It
will be a lot easier than trying to load all this in the car and then
take it up four flights of stairs to our apartment."

Eve, who had been looking up at the tall buildings, was
terrified at the suggestion.

"Check it? I don't think I could sleep worrying about it," she
said, shocked.

"OK," Rita said, still recovering from the excitement of the
greeting, "we'll try to get it in the car."

With Eve directing, Rita and Gary loaded the car. There were
suitcases and boxes everywhere. On laps. On their shoulders.
They made conversation on the way home, but the shifting and
falling boxes were really the main event of the ride.

As soon as Rita and Gary got to the apartment in the West
Village and dragged the suitcases and boxes up the stairs and
into their living room, Eve anxiously asked if she could use the
telephone.

"Of course," Rita said. "Do you have some friends to call while you're here? If you do, feel free to invite them over."

"No, I'd like to call Amsterdam to tell Ivan that I'll be on tomorrow's flight from New York."

Nowhere in Rita's conscious mind did she expect to pay for this call. But when Rita heard her cousin ask the long distance operator for a number in Amsterdam without saying that she wanted to reverse the charges, her consciousness began to sharpen.

"Well," Rita rationalized, "she'll probably take care of that later, and anyway, how often do I see her?"

Fifteen minutes later, when Eve got off the phone, the three sat down and talked for an hour and a half. They caught up on a lifetime of not knowing each other. Through the entire conversation Eve kept coming back to how wonderful it was to find Rita and Gary at home. (It was Friday and they did have other plans but cancelled them after Eve called.) And how wonderful they were to pick her up and ease her through the difficulties and dangers of New York.

"How about dinner?" they asked. "Where would you like to go? What kind of food would you like?" They wanted to be good hosts.

The truth was that Eve was dressed like a European refugee from the Second World War and that limited where they could go. From their conversation it was obvious to Rita that Eve was "dressing down," her clothes and effects not truly a reflection of her financial realities or social position, but simply part of her image.

"A restaurant?" Eve responded. "I really can't afford a restaurant."

"Please. You're our guest," Rita said reflexively, embarrassed that Eve could have thought they would let her pay for her dinner.

"Well, if we're going out, I have a problem. I don't eat meat. Do you know of a vegetarian restaurant?"

Rita and Gary's connection with vegetarian restaurants was limited, since both of them were devoted carnivores who considered a vegetarian restaurant a contradiction in terms.

"And besides," Eve added, just beginning to warm up, "I really wouldn't be comfortable in any place—you know—fancy." With that statement she began wandering through the rooms of the apartment. She commented from one of the rooms over to the front room, where Gary and Rita were still sitting, "Part of the joy of living in Europe is living with simplicity, free of all the 'things' Americans find so necessary."

Coming back into the living room she remarked with disdain, "My God, you have *two* TV sets. You're really Americans, I can see." Eve laughed. She hadn't watched television since she was a teenager. "In Amsterdam," she explained, "we don't even have a television."

Rita wasn't one to tolerate anyone doing an ugly-American number on her, especially a fellow American, however expatriate and however related. As Eve's conversation became more trendy and anti-American-way-of-life Gary and Rita became more openly indignant. Finally they excused themselves for a few minutes to "clean up" and showed Eve where she would sleep.

In the privacy of their bedroom they discussed the situation and decided they would not deposit her down the dumbwaiter or even politely suggest that she find a more comfortable room in a nearby cheap hotel. They decided to stick it out. There would only be one visit from Eve in their lifetime and this was it. They agreed that they could take anything for so short a time. Besides, at this point, they were getting curious about how far Eve's absurdities would go.

They remembered a "hippy gourmet" restaurant in the East Village and went there for dinner. It was strictly incense and brown rice. Eve was finally at home. They had their Kama Sutra salads and strolled back to the apartment in the West Village.

By now Eve had got hold of herself and once more apologized for being such a bother and expecting so much on so little notice. Rita and Gary were really wonderful again. But, though they were okay, even if carnivorous and owners of two TV's, Eve discouraged them from pointing out any of the landmarks or points of interest they passed. New York depressed her and she just wasn't interested in its buildings. The three finally made it back home and up the stairs.

Once inside Eve mentioned that she was "low on dollars" and might have to find a place to cash a traveller's check. It was ten thirty at night. The only places that Rita thought might cash the check were the liquor store, drug store, or the market.

"Do you think they'll accept one of these?" asked Eve, pulling out an obscure traveller's check from a bank in Holland.

"Oh, boy, I don't think *any* place will cash *this*," Rita remarked, "but you don't have too much to worry about. You'll be back in Holland tomorrow and I guess you won't be needing anything for restaurants or hotels."

"Well," Eve insisted, "I think I must have about twenty dollars."

Gary took out twenty dollars and gave it to her.

"You know," said Eve, pocketing the money as she headed towards the bed Rita was making up for her, "I must pick up my tickets in the morning."

"Really? Where?"

"At the ticket office in midtown."

It was eight thirty in the morning when Gary loaded a disappointed Eve with her suitcases and boxes into a passing cab. Her plane was to leave at two in the afternoon, but Eve wanted to be certain she had enough time, "because departures always ended up being so complicated."

As they said their goodbyes, Eve already in the cab, she called out one passing request.

"Would you call the family and tell them goodbye for me?"

"The family?" Rita asked feebly.

"Yes," she answered out the window as the cab moved off. "In California."

She was gone. It was as though some heavy net had been dropped over them and now they were free.

"You know?" Rita said to Gary over their morning coffee, "this odyssey started with four innocent words: 'Why don't we meet?' "

"I guess you're not going to call the family in California." Gary laughed.

"Yeah, Gary, I guess I'm not." Now they both laughed.

Suddenly Rita became solemn.

"What's wrong?" Gary asked.

"Look over there." Rita pointed as Gary got up to see what she was pointing at from her side of the table.

There they were. Two small boxes stuck behind the door. Two boxes carefully addressed to Eve in Holland.

The Closet Competitor

The Closet Competitor doesn't want to see himself as a competitive person, so he keeps his acts of competition hidden in the closet. He resorts to passively violent competition in order to maintain his image as cooperative, not competitive, because he sees these traits as mutually exclusive.

The Closet Competitor's technique is to devalue the achievements of people by denying or distorting them, "one-upping" them while staying out of any direct competition.

A Closet Competitor always steals your thunder. His methods may vary, but the person he competes with ends up feeling discounted and his achievements or talents devalued.

If the competitor's target has just closed a deal, won an award, or been elected to some office, the Closet Competitor will often respond to the news with a story about *his* experiences in the same area. They are often much less significant. The Closet Competitor will relate these somewhat similar experiences ostensibly to show that he appreciates and understands the target's position. But it is really his way of erasing the target's moment of success.

Closet Competitors will never say, "You think *that's* something; let me tell you about my deal, (award, election)." That would be open competition. He would say instead, "Oh, how wonderful. I'm so happy for you. I know just how it must feel to get the Pulitzer Prize. In high school I once got a journalism award myself."

Whatever his tactics, the Closet Competitor takes the joy out of winning and can make an announcement of accomplishment uncomfortable. The target who touches off the Closet Competitor can be made to feel disoriented or embarrassed by bringing up his accomplishment, protective toward the Closet Competitor (by sensing his discomfort), or too boastful and egotistic.

Sara wasn't like other unpublished fiction writers. She seemed to have the drive of five people, coming home after her job at the bakery and banging out pages until early in the morning. She was always anxious to write. While others had one reason or another for not getting things down on paper, Sara never had any problem. She didn't feel quite alive unless she had done some writing during the day.

People who read a great deal and saw her material knew that it was only a matter of time before her stories would be the source of dinner table talk. Sara, who had submitted a few things to publishers, seemed more interested in writing than in having her things published. For hours she would bang out mysteries, stories with multiple twists and minimal gore filling sheet after sheet of paper.

An admirer of Sara's stories took it upon herself to submit one of them to a magazine. Since Sara was not pushing herself to be published, the admirer thought she would give her a boost. The publisher bought the story. In fact, the editors were so pleased about it that they decided to make her story the feature of the month and commissioned a well-known illustrator to design the cover of the magazine. This was an honor the magazine had reserved over the years. Only a few other times had it featured unknown writers on its cover.

When Sara received an advance copy of the magazine she was ecstatic. Until then she had felt that maybe—just maybe—this was all a dream. It wouldn't work out somehow. It was just too unusual. But the magazine surpassed even her admirer's expectations. The colors on the cover, the layout, the entire handling of the story was magnificent.

That night Sara's mother, who had been kept in the dark about the magazine publication (as had most of Sara's friends, since she kept thinking that something might happen and her story wouldn't be published) dropped by unexpectedly. A publicist of little note, her smile was as thin as a 1973 Watergate cover story when she saw her daughter's triumph. "How marvelous, dear," she said as she turned to the door. "Just fabulous." She opened the door. "Be right back," she shouted as she ran down the steps to her car, leaving the apartment door open. Sara couldn't figure out what her mother could be getting. She waited, puzzled.

Mom ran back into the apartment with one hand in her familiar briefcase, stocked with her pictures and resumés. As she pulled out a yellowing article from a small town paper she glossed over her daughter's achievement with another "Gee, that's so wonderful, dear," and then squealed, "Now, you're not the only one in the family who writes. Look at this from Your Mother the Publicist." She handed Sara the newsclip, dated three weeks before. It was about a radio personality who would be attending the coming Harvest Moon Ball at a dude ranch just outside Pinball City. The six lines of unbylined copy were buried near the obituaries. Sara's mother had equated her daughter's 25,000-word piece of fiction, featured and illustrated, with her six lines of blabber.

"See," Mom said, bulldozing her daughter to ground level, "it's what I've always said. This is a family with creative talent. A two-writer family."

The Fortress

The Fortress gives the impression that he has something important to say, something to give to a relationship, if only someone will try to scale his wall. Anyone who accepts the challenge and makes the attempt is frustrated. The ladder is pushed off, sending the target crashing to the ground.

One of the Fortress's favorite deceptions is to seduce his prey into sharing his most private thoughts or personal secrets. Once the prey has revealed himself and is vulnerable and exposed, the Fortress withholds and reveals nothing. The seduced victim becomes hurt or angry as the Fortress retreats farther behind a wall, still sending signals for the victim to try again.

FORTRESS I

He wasn't talking, but Tina knew that something was wrong. Nothing you could put your finger on. He hadn't said a word. But when you live with someone as long as she had lived with Alan, you know.

It had been a spectacularly good week for Tina. She'd been promoted to account executive and was handling some of the biggest accounts in the agency. She'd always wanted to make a place for herself in advertising and it looked as if she was finally going to reach her goal. Another couple of years, she thought, and she'd be off on her own.

Her main worry was Alan. He just wasn't getting anywhere in the English department, wasn't making the right friends, wasn't getting the best class assignments. He would be up for tenure this year and he had reason to be anxious.

Tina knew that she could always support the two of them if he had to leave City College and find a teaching job somewhere else. She never brought it up but it was comforting to know that her success had given the two of them this security, even if it wasn't going to be openly acknowledged.

"Alan's a good teacher," Tina thought, "and just needs some time to figure out the politics of academia." He was, after all, a leading authority on Henry James and, as soon as he finished the book he'd been working on for the last five years, the world of letters would be open to him.

Tina was confident. Alan, on the other hand, spent most of his time with Tina either dropping incomplete sentences about wanting "to just pick up and get the hell away from here" or being totally uncommunicative, sitting in front of the television set consuming the frequent sports events that were getting more and more of his attention.

Tonight he hadn't said a word.

Tina didn't feel free to leave Alan alone. She felt compelled to try to get whatever problems there were out in the open so they could at least share them.

"Alan—" Tina approached cautiously, "I'd like to talk to you."

No answer.

"Alan, don't you think it would be a good idea if we could talk out some of the problems?"

"Oh, God, I wish I could," said Alan.

"Then just do it. Tell me. We can work out whatever is wrong."

"If only I could . . ." Alan began.

"What? If you could what, Alan?" Tina persisted in asking.

"I don't know." Alan didn't take his eyes from the basketball game on the tube.

"Would you like to talk about it or do you just want to be alone?" Tina asked.

"I guess . . . I don't know . . . if only I could just . . ."

"Just *what*? What is it?"

The room was silent except for the fast-paced commentary from the television.

"Alan?" Tina asked again.

No answer.

"Hey, Alan, c'mon. What is it? Is it something I did? Please, Alan, would you turn off that thing and let's talk. Let's at least *try* to talk."

"I'd really like to but I can't."

"Can you please *try* to tell me what's the matter? We don't have to talk about it. I'm just so worried about you."

Silence.

"Hey, Alan, c'mon. What's the matter?"

"Nothing," Alan said with more emphasis than he had exerted in a long time. "It's really nothing."

FORTRESS II

AUTHOR'S NOTE

*Having read the original manuscript of "*THE NEW MEN'S LIB: HANDS OFF!*" by Francis J. Moriarty, it is clear that the edited version, which appears here as it did in the* Los Angeles Times, *misrepresents the author's intent. Therefore, this article is not only an example of a Fortress but also an illustration of Idea Warping (see Part III).*

I have a friend who considers herself a militant feminist. Right now she is unhappy. A *man* is involved. He keeps rejecting her.

"He could be something more to me than just another friend," she says, "and I haven't felt that way about a man in over five years."

Why she has not felt that way is not particularly important here. Nor is there anything novel about love spurned. What is important is that something indeed novel has been happening— new to her and to an increasingly large number of her female friends. She is a victim of Going Without.

Which is not without its irony. For some time now she and many of her sisters have done without men. They have fought, rightly, for a space of their own, and from it they started a critical reappraisal of sex and sex roles.

In creating a critique of women's social position, they have necessarily looked carefully at men and have exhaustively catalogued all the faults with traditional maleness. A lot of men—some kicking and screaming—have come to accept the need for radical change. Now a number of women who have been at the forefront are willing, even eager, to reestablish closer ties with the opposite sex. But at this critical juncture it appears that some of the men are not so ready.

"What the hell is *wrong* with men?" says this woman I know. "They keep saying, like this male friend of mine, 'I want a woman who would like to be President of the United States and still get a kick out of changing diapers.' So I say, in effect, 'Okay, here I am. I mean, I'm ready. It's taken me a long time to get here, but if you want it, you've got it.' So what the hell does he say? 'I'm sorry, but you're too much of a woman for me.'

"Now where the hell does this leave *me*? If I'm passive, I'm undesirable. If I'm strong, I'm so desirable he can't handle it."

So the problem is *his*, not hers; *ours*, not theirs. He is saying "No," as are more and more men of all ages, and I can understand it. As she speaks, I can feel growing within me a sense of real pleasure at being among the rejectors, not one of the rejected.

True, men always had the power to define what they thought was beautiful and to reject individual women on that basis—a cruel game based on invidious distinctions. But now men are choosing, some of us, to reject the whole group.

Too many of us males, I suspect, have spent too much of our lives playing the Friday-night adolescent, circling the dance floor, full of fright, pretending we were picking our prey. We have welcomed women's liberation, I think, not because we perceived women as victims of injustice but because we sensed an advantage for ourselves in supporting the movement.

We secretly rejoiced in the distance women have put between us, and now we are loath to give it up. That distance has given each of us a place to breathe and think, a place we probably never would have sought for ourselves. The great weight of play-acting has been lifted from us, and, in reaching for control over our own sex role, we are gaining a power over sex itself.

If this is a power trip, Going Without is one manisfestation of our power. Maybe the shift toward both bi- and homosexuality is not at all a sign of expanding sexual horizons; maybe it is a sign that many people are seeing themselves as androgynous or even genderless—and implicit in the possibility of being *Either* is the power to be *Neither*.

If all this were only a cycle—if we could feel confidently that men and women would end up together again, albeit on new terms—then we could note and dismiss our new-found abstemiousness. But it is not so simple as that. Going Without is certainly not a fad, limited just to a few males from the elite stratum of society. It ties in, for example, with the strong '60s influence of Oriental philosophy. It makes ecological sense, for it provides wonderfully effective birth control and efficient recycling of energy. Its highest manifestation is the latest political catch phrase: Less is More.

If less is indeed more, then it ought to follow that Nothing is Everything. Going Without means Getting It All. Women are objects? All right, I'll make *me* the object, but I'll do it without being oppressive. Sexually speaking, I'll just disappear.

Power through rejection and control: That's the sum of it. Though not widely articulated, this approach may help explain the vast popularity of Jerry Brown, our handsome bachelor-governor with global aspirations but monastic tastes. Brown has raised Going Without to the level of art, and in so doing has helped to define a widely perceived need to control personal appetites as a key step in the process of turning around an over-indulgent society. Indeed, he has apparently won converts by the thousands to his vision of "lowered expectations."

Since sex is as ubiquitous as the next toothpaste commercial, it only makes sense for sex to be the first to give way. But men are discovering that sex is a lot more complex than we had imagined. Women warned us of this, and they were right.

So long as men participated in a game for which they largely wrote the rules, there was little need or time for reflection. Now some of us have felt the need and gained the time, courtesy of feminism. Just as we see women differently, so we also see ourselves in a new perspective.

A magazine writer recently asked why men "can't get a straight male act together" anymore. The reason, it seems to me, is that our "straight male act" was based upon a superiority that women no longer grant us and that we no longer ascribe ourselves.

If we want to abolish discrimination, both cultural and legal, based on genital differences, the only sure way is to transcend the female/male distinction.

Meanwhile members of each sex have increasingly come to stand at opposite ends of the room. As we warily eye one another, uncertain what move to make, many of us are just Going Without.

The Blackmailer

The Blackmailer waits until his target is in a vulnerable position or is faced with a difficult decision, most often in a situation the Blackmailer has created. He then threatens to withdraw support or weaken his target unless the target agrees to his demands. The Blackmailer is a master of timing and the skillful use of guilt.

BLACKMAILER I

"Let's see," said Frank. "My bill comes to $6.25. I've got four . . . five . . . six . . ." Frank stopped. "Hey, Bob, you got a quarter?"

Bob was expecting it. Whenever the checks came he would take out money to pay for himself, then he would instinctively put his hand back in his pocket, groping for change, waiting for Frank to ask.

It was an old pattern, something that was part of their weekly dinners together for a few years now. At first, they hadn't mentioned it at all. It was only twenty or thirty cents. Nothing to make an issue about. Then it became a joke, something that Frank would laugh at when Bob would bring it up just before the checks arrived.

"Yeah," Bob finally answered, "I've got a quarter. Here."

"By the way," Frank went on, "could you take the tip? I'll settle up with you later."

"Um hm," said Bob, nodding. "I won't hold my breath."

"What't the big thing, Bob? It's only some change."

That's all it ever was—"just change"—but Bob was beginning to be irritated by it, the joke was wearing thin. Still, he left the tip.

Bob had recently begun to notice that Frank was *always* chipping away at his change. No big transactions, no "loans," just a constant expectation that Bob would always come through with those necessary few cents that Frank always needed.

Bob liked Frank. They'd been friends a long time. But he didn't

94

like the role of change dropper. So the next time they met for dinner, he decided, he was going to put an end to it.

Sure enough, when the checks came, Bob found himself reaching automatically into his pocket. Then he caught himself, took out just enough for his check and his part of the tip, left it on the table, and started to leave.

"Hey, Bob," Frank called predictably. "Can you believe that I'm short two cents? I've got $5.25 and my bill is $5.27. Let me have two cents."

"No," Bob said, "I don't have two cents. I don't have any change."

"Sure you have some change. I saw you get some when we stopped for cigarettes. Come on. Stop kiddin' around and let me have the pennies."

"No," said Bob firmly. "Maybe I do have two cents, but I'm damn sick and tired of always putting out the nickels and dimes for you. If you add up all the money it isn't a small amount anymore, but what's more important is that I just don't want you to always hold me up for the change."

"I don't believe this," Frank responded without a pause. "You mean to say that you're going to jeopardize our whole friendship over a lousy two cents?"

BLACKMAILER II

After paying the contractor Sherry found out that he had installed the drains wrong and the water was running through the ceiling in the den. That was only the beginning. Almost everything the builders had done was incomplete, inadequate, or illegal. She called S&M Builders to get them to come back and make good on their contract, but they never came. She went to the State Board of Contractors, but they said they were helpless to get her money back. Sherry concluded that the only way she was going to recover the money was to sue. She called Ronald Hinkle, a lawyer someone had recommended. He met with her and took all the necessary information, plus a check towards his fee and expenses.

A lot of time passed and Sherry heard nothing. When she called Hinkle he was never in and he didn't return her calls. Finally, after six or seven tries, she reached him. He told her that he would be filing the suit the next day, coincidentally, and would keep her informed about any depositions or court dates.

A few months later Sherry got a notice of default in the mail. S&M Builders, it seemed, had countersued when they had received her suit. The original papers had gone to Hinkle, who hadn't told Sherry. Now S&M were claiming that since she hadn't responded they were entitled to a judgment by default. Sherry was furious and called Hinkle.

"What is this I got in the mail?" Sherry said excitedly. "I didn't even know they answered our complaint, much less countered it with a phony law suit."

"Don't panic," Hinkle said reassuringly. "That's exactly what I thought when I got their answer. I thought it was a fake too and I didn't take it seriously. Anyway, I was out of town when the day came to answer their countersuit and I gave it to my secretary to file with the court. She must have forgotten. But don't worry. I'll make a motion to set aside the judgment and tell them that I was away on another case. Don't worry about a thing. I'll take care of it."

"God, I hope so. I can't believe that we don't have a judgment against *them* already and they have one against *me*. Do you know how unfair that is?"

"Look, Sherry. No use getting mad about it. I'll just do what needs to be done and everything will be OK," Hinkle said without emotion.

"Well, OK. As long as you can set it straight. This thing has been going on for a long time now. I had to pay for the same work twice and I have to pay you too. So I am more than a little bit concerned."

"Don't be such a worrier," said Hinkle.

Almost a month passed before Sherry heard from Hinkle again. This time his voice was less casual.

"I hate to tell you this," Hinkle started ominously, "but the judge wouldn't accept my motion to set aside the judgment without a hearing. He's set a hearing date a week from today. Can you make it?"

"You mean I have to take a day off work and come downtown because of your mistake? Why do I have to be there?"

"Well, you don't have to be there, but then the judge won't listen to my arguments about the judgment. Whose fault it is isn't here nor there." Hinkle was becoming emotional.

So was Sherry. "This should be *your* problem, not mine," she said. "I paid you to take care of things correctly. I can't help it if your secretary does this or you don't do that. Why should I have to take additional time to deal with this?"

"Well, you don't," said Hinkle indignantly. "And I don't have to represent you either, if that's how you feel."

The Reluctant Champ

The Reluctant Champ avoids the isolation and responsibility of being a winner by denying he is one.

Actually, there are two varieties of Reluctant Champ. One is afraid of letting his power be known and used. The other is simply afraid of having it. The first feigns powerlessness to avoid the burdens and responsibility that come with power. His only fear is that his power will seem accessible to people or causes when he wants it all for himself.

The second rejects the winner's role out of fear of isolation and separation. He is afraid, even though he has "won," of losing his identity as one of "the people."

The Reluctant Champ, whether motivated by "elitism" or "populism," rejects the image of power and in the process denies others whatever influence he may have. Since most people expect power to be used constructively in their behalf, both denials make them disillusioned and resentful.

The "guilty" Reluctant Champ apologizes for winning and degrades his position. The "jealous" Reluctant Champ maintains all the trappings of power but refuses to share it. In doing so he provokes his expectant constituency.

Either way the Reluctant Champ masks his power so it becomes ineffective. People then are victimized by the Reluctant Champ's pretence at victimization.

Roger Holmes was the president of the largest bank in a midwestern city. He had worked his way up from operations manager, even though his father had been president of the bank before him. He didn't want anyone to think he had inherited his position. Roger Holmes had worked for it. He deserved to be where he was.

As rewarding as his work was to him, it did bring with it some unfortunate sacrifices. The main thing he had given up was being close to his children. There just wasn't enough time to keep the bank number one and still give his kids the time he knew they needed. Roger Holmes wished there was some way he could make the day long enough for all the things that were expected of him. He settled for the realization that he couldn't.

So it was with some excitement that Roger Holmes heard over his intercom that two of his children were there in the bank to see him and that they had brought some friends along. Roger had the children shown into his magnificent office.

"We've come to ask your help, Father," said his youngest child, Christopher, thirteen. "We're trying to get a petition together to start a teen center in Northport so we have some place to go without getting thrown out of the pizza place all the time or being hassled by the cops. We thought that since you knew everybody on the town council they'd listen to you. So we'd like you to give them the petitions once they're all signed."

The children waited for Roger's response. His middle daughter, Andrea, fifteen, was straining for the answer, leaning forward in her chair. The others smiled and were silent.

The intercom buzzed. Roger Holmes picked up the phone.

"Yes. Tell him I'll call him back. Call the mayor and tell him I'll be a few minutes late for lunch. Then, no more calls or interruptions, please, Mrs. Neal."

He put down the phone and looked at the kids, five of them, from twelve to fifteen years old, still waiting for his answer.

"I'd like to help you if I could," he said, "but what makes you think they'll listen to me any more than anyone else?"

There was no answer.

Roger Holmes wanted to be sure he made himself clear.

"I think what you're doing is worthwhile, and I'm glad to see all you kids working together like this. I just don't see how I can help you. After all, who am I?" Roger Holmes smiled, then got up to keep his lunch date like any other working man.

The Gentle Provocateur

The Gentle Provocateur can say, "Have a nice day," when his target has just told him that he is about to go to the dentist for root canal work. The Gentle Provocateur may offer a piece of cake to a person he knows is having a hard time dieting. When the dieter angrily refuses, the Gentle Provocateur feels victimized and makes the dieter feel guilty for refusing. He would make offhand remarks about a social or political issue to someone he knows is especially vulnerable about the subject.

The Gentle Provocateur provokes for the pleasure of immediate antagonism. He would, for instance, invite an actor who missed getting the lead part in a play to the cast party. He is commonly known as a skillful button pusher.

In the fifties, when Abe got home from work, he would ask his son Jerry, "How did the Giants do?" Actually, he didn't ask Jerry about the Giants every day, just on the evenings that followed a Giant loss. It wasn't the nicest question to ask Jerry then. The walls in his room were lined with pictures of the various ballplayers who made up the New York team. Willie Mays, Monte Irvin, Whitey Lockman all grinned toothily from their places on his bedroom walls.

Jerry's every waking thought was of the Giants. They were his friends, his family, his life.

Jerry took Giants' losses very badly. Once he was watching a game the Giants were winning. After the first eight innings the score was 4–2. It seemed they'd have an easy victory. Suddenly, with two out in the ninth inning, someone from the other team hit a three-run homer, beating the Giants, 5–4. After the last out of the game Jerry went into a rage. He threw pillows, crayons, cards, and magazines. Everything portable in the house went flying through the air. Running out of lightweight objects, Jerry yanked on the coffee table and, surprising himself with his ten-year-old manliness, pulled a leg right off.

That stopped him. His face flushed. Jerry was imagining what his mother was going to do when she found a three-legged coffee table in her living room. He ran to the hardware store, used the remnants of his allowance to buy glue, then ran back home to set the broken leg.

That night, Abe came home just after Jerry had finished Molly's, his mother's, special chocolate cake. Although Abe was tired, he smiled as he walked into the kitchen and pinched Jerry's cheek. Jerry knew what was coming. He braced himself.

"How did the Giants do today?" his father asked in mock innocence.

"Abe, please," Molly interjected, knowing from years of experience what was brewing. "If the Giants lost, why must you bother the boy?" Then turning to her son, she said, "Jerry, don't listen to him. Go ahead. You're finished with your cake. Go in the living room and wait for Wild Bill Hickock to come on television."

A half hour later, after Wild Bill had put all the bad guys in jail, Abe walked in on Jerry.

"I saw Sam Fuchs today. He says that Ollie Matson is a better football player than Frank Gifford." Abe knew that Gifford of the New York (football) Giants was Jerry's favorite football player. It was part of Abe's ritual to tease Jerry during the baseball season by saying that both Mickey Mantle of the Yankees and Duke Snider of the Dodgers were better than Jerry's all-time hero, Willie Mays, and, during football time, that Matson was better than Gifford. Now, in mid-September, with football around the corner, he was pulling out his football tease again.

"He is not," Jerry whined, not really wanting to get into another argument with his father.

"What do you mean he's not? Sam Fuchs says he is and Sam Fuchs played football. Who should I believe, you or Sam Fuchs?"

"Me," his son said.

"You?" Abe was pushing him. "You don't even know the score of today's Giant game. By the way, what was that score?"

With that Jerry moved towards the coffee table. He put

his right knee against the broken table leg and pushed gently. The table leg gave out and the whole thing crashed to the floor.

"Molly, come in here," Abe called. "Look what your son did."

Jerry didn't get to see any other shows that night. Molly gave him a hell of a beating while Abe watched Jackie Gleason.

III

Our New Society
Sheep Without Shepherds

The Incredible Shrinking Man

Nationalism, the sense of "us" that was the idealized America, has diminished to "me."

I am my own frontier. You are alien country.

We have become isolationists who live in close quarters. We appear not to invade one another, while diplomatically (with all that word's implications of foreign intrigue) we take as much space as we can get. The New Expansionism is psychic *lebensraum,* the surreptitious invasion of the borders of others.

"All our surveys over the last decade," says New York pollster Daniel Yankelovitch, "show that more and more people are coming to believe that the part of their lives that they are able to control is diminishing. As individual autonomy is shrunk by the actions of government and institutions we become more determined to control the remainder."

Disillusioned about our decreasing influence and convinced that we are inadequate to cope with the outside world, we leave control in the hands of fewer and larger conglomerates of vested interests. Lacking even a cohesive family to reinforce our strengths, we give up our capacity to resist the control of giant bureaucracies or the influence of special interest groups. We constantly remake ourselves in therapies or self-help movements so that we may be better able to handle the world. At the very same time "the world" is becoming better able to handle us.

We have voluntarily given up more power than any government, conglomerate, or multinational corporation could have taken from us had we resisted. As political and environmental conditions worsen, people dissipate their stress and anger with deep breathing or jogging to maintain personal "equilibrium." These and other stress-reducing, "meditative" solutions enable us to function better in a bureaucratic culture. They also make us willing participants in the status quo. Social non-responsiveness has become our psychological adaptation to our covertly imposed serfdom.

Columnist Jack Anderson writes about the Internal Revenue

Service and "the taxpayers in modern America (who) have been brought into bondage with a finesse so unobtrusive that they may not have noticed it."

In our helplessness we have allowed intrusions that have produced social upheavals in the not too distant past. Anderson elaborates: "The crude attempts of the czars to raise revenues often provoked bloody resistance. Internal Revenue perpetrates the same atrocities peaceably and effortlessly."

People have not only given into the excesses and intrusions of government but have also allowed their privacy to be slowly and effectively destroyed.

A few years ago a Senate committee found that there were 858 government data banks with 1.2 billion records in fifty-four agencies. They reported that at least twenty-nine of these data banks were established to collect derogatory material on individuals. They also reported that half of the 858 data banks *had no statutory authority for their existence.*

Granted that a complex technological society must keep records and collect a great deal of information to make it run, that same process, unchecked, destroys personal privacy and autonomy. This destruction has not made people feel angry so much as vulnerable. They don't feel they can get together and fight back. The enemy is lurking everywhere. They feel helpless.

The information that corporate and governmental data banks hold on each citizen is not only excessive but often incorrect, treacherous, and easily accessible. With medical, educational, armed service, motor vehicle, civil, criminal, political, real estate, credit, bank, and other records easily available to anyone with the will to get them, it's easy to understand how vulnerable most people feel. We are feeling the fragility of our "private lives." That an unconfirmed remark from a neighbor may determine a person's credit or job rating only reinforces our senses of vulnerability and futility.

This loss of autonomy and privacy didn't result from a sudden sneak attack by a foreign enemy. It is the result of thousands of small intrusions over many years that collectively have eroded individual liberties. It is also the result of thousands of small concessions and non-responses by people who never knew what their inaction would produce. We didn't actually lose our autonomy. We let it be taken away.

The enemy isn't the government or the corporations or "the system." The enemy is our passivity. It has made us smaller and less able to resist.

Passivity has made us isolated and angry and more than a little crazy. But despite all the evidence of what our personal and national passivity has created, we hold onto it. Many people value it. Education perpetuates it. Social welfare demands it.

Some time ago I remember laughing at a newspaper cartoon before the painful feeling of recognition made it no longer funny. It showed a driver at the end of a road. In front of him were a maze of signs.

"No Parking."

"No Left Turn."

"No Right Turn."

"No U Turn."

"No Standing."

"No Trespassing."

"Violators will be Prosecuted."

This reflects the internal condition of many people. They can't move and they can't stand still.

Studies in neurosis and the development of psychotic behavior have used this experiment. Maze-wise rats are punished randomly and not allowed a safe place to hide. After a short time, a few hours perhaps, the rats just stand still and accept their random shocks. They behave erratically for a while. They may even bite. But they invariably become passive. They learn to accept their helplessness and just sit, defecate, and wait for the next shock. No one so far has devised a way to communicate with the rats and ask them what's going on, but from their behavior they seem to drop out and turn off. The shocks, even when they reach life-threatening levels, stop having any perceptible effect.

Not being rats, humans can analyze and react to physical or psychological attacks. Sometimes overt violence is the best reaction. Under other conditions sabotage is called for. But when neither the enemy nor the attack is visible, or when our ability to strike back effectively is virtually non-existent, we, like the rat, may drop out, turn off, and give up. Under these dangerous conditions, most people simply retreat into themselves and the uncomfortable safety of immobility.

Many of our present struggles are with "invisible enemies." These enemies have affected the mentality of so many people that psychologists have created a whole new area of study they call "learned helplessness" which deals with the ways people acquire and maintain self-images as victims.

It may be possible to regain some of the power lost to "invisible enemies" by making them visible, giving them an identity, and giving ourselves some idea of how they affect us and our society.

We know that the Flock is part of this adversary force, assaulting our psyches daily and giving birth to communal tension. But invisible enemies can also be embodied in processes as well as people, in power structures and their power symbols.

We can see the amorphous aggression of Violent Sheep take shape by studying the process I call "leveling," the use of what I describe as "idea warping," the power structure I define as "the expertocracy," and the power symbols I see standing in place of leadership and old-fashioned inspirational heroes.

This combination of people and process has created a society that is afraid of itself. Like the small child in the dark, we may get some needed courage and rational support by turning the light on our shadowy fears.

Leveling: Making the Piper Pay

Leveling, bringing someone down, "cutting him down to size," doesn't appear in our lexicon of violent words even though it's always been with us. The person who stands above the crowd has always stood there at his own risk, a ready target for jealous competitors looking to take his place. It's common knowledge that unveiled power or success is an open invitation to attack. Throughout history anyone who proclaimed himself a "top gun" also became a prime target for anyone in the public who saw himself as a contender to the title. That sort of covetous, open leveling is an old story.

We live in a culture that not only assumes that power corrupts but has also deduced from that assumption that being powerless is more virtuous than being powerful. Consequently, whatever jealousy may lurk deep in the mind of the leveler, he rarely takes over power once it has been leveled. Leveling is an end in itself.

Those who try and then fail are more trusted than those who succeed. It's easier to identify with them. They're more like "the rest of us."

The general response to anyone who openly admits or aspires to power or competence is to withhold support, even when it is obvious that he needs it. Violent passivity becomes a leveling device. The more competent a person lets himself appear, the less help he gets from anyone. This is his penalty: He is left alone to take care of himself.

Attacks on the publicly successful are often highly organized. All but the most extreme physical attacks on "stars" are not only socially acceptable but have become cultural pastimes encouraged by the media.

Rock musicians and superstars are consumed by their audiences, who demand such intensity in their performances that longevity is improbable. The rare exceptions who survive are forced to devise such complex means of self-protection that they are often prisoners of the very public that "adores" them.

Isolation and loneliness have become standard dues for public success.

No wonder then that the six-year-old son of a friend of mine emphatically rejected his teacher's attempt to place him in a special class for the "gifted": "They'll just ask me to do more stuff. Then I'll do it. Then they'll give me more. And more. I'll be doing more work than the regular kids all the time. I don't want to be different. I want to be just regular like my friends."

When six year olds show this kind of understanding of the burdens of "superiority," the future of mediocrity seems assured. The boy had learned from only two years of teacher and peer pressure that being special was not worth the "rewards."

Peer pressure is what my friend Jean felt when she called May with some good news. Here's the conversation she relayed to me.

"Hi, May?"

"Yeah," May answered.

"How are you doing?"

"Oh, fine."

"Guess what."

"What, honey, what's up?"

"You'll never guess," Jean teased her.

"C'mon, what?" May laughed.

"I got it. I got the job!"

"Oh, no kidding," May said, suddenly distracted.

Jean didn't pick up May's distraction. "Yeah, can you believe it? Not only that but they're gonna give me the salary I asked for."

"Wow." Then silence.

"Isn't that something? God, I'm so excited," Jean repeated into the silence.

"I'll bet." May sounded a little depressed.

"I can't believe it." Jean is really talking to herself.

"I'll bet," May unexcitedly repeated.

"I never thought this could happen." Jean started to try to explain her excitement. "It was just such a surprise."

"I know." May seemed to be eating something.

"Wowee," Jean continued.

Silence.

"So, what's happening with you?" Jean changed the subject as it became apparent that her news was going nowhere.

"Oh, nothing, as usual," May sighed. "I guess that's why I feel kind of depressed."

"Aw, gee, May. That's too bad. Anything I can do?"

"I don't think so."

"C'mon. I'll take you out for dinner."

"No, I don't want to dampen your evening."

"Aw, c'mon . . ."

"Naw, I don't feel like doing much of anything," May moaned.

By the time Jean hung up, her excitement was gone and low-level depression had set in. "It's strange," she thought to herself, "I felt so good just a few minutes ago."

Leveling is a passively violent tactic that keeps the flock intact and its sheep in comfortable equilibrium. When directed at the stray it can make it feel guilt, panic, and disorientation—all prerequisites for failure. It accounts for the high mortality rate among successful strays and the reason most people are satisfied—even eager—to be "regular" like everyone else.

Leveling enforces conformity and preserves the power of the group. It depends on an unwritten law that applies equally to the junkie and the genius: it's OK to better yourself as long as you don't get better than the rest of us. The law and its implied violence is justified by a warped idea of democracy and equality which says that everyone has the right to make it big but no one should make it so big that he shows up his friends.

"*Rocky* was successful for the same reason as *Roots* and *Easter*," social critic and comedian Dick Gregory said. "The underdog *almost* wins. If Rocky'd knocked that nigger out in the first round, or Christ jumped off the cross, nothin' would've happened."

When artist Andy Warhol predicted that in the not too distant future everyone would have fifteen minutes of fame, he did more than satirize the speed at which we consume stars and leaders. He was also pointing out the limitations we put on leadership and stardom.

Comedian Richard Pryor talks about everyday "down home"

leveling when he describes going back to his old block after he became successful.

"Some brothers break my face. 'Nigger,' they say, 'you ain't shit. You wasn't shit when you was here. That's [his comedy routines] the same shit you done around the pool room. It wasn't nothin'. Lemme have a dollar.' "

Like many tactics of psychological warfare, leveling has its roots in our national character, particularly as that character unfolded in the late 1940's.

Dr. Margaret Mead once told me that she believed there were only two distinct generations alive today: those people born before the atom bomb and those people born after it. The social and psychological conditions that separate these generations are not reconcilable; there is a fault in the sociological and anthropological crust that will never come together. Out of this schism, this critical psychological separation, passively violent leveling evolved. It began with the leveling of American power and leadership after the Second World War—the putting down of a power never before known on earth.

In a few short years after World War II ended with the use of atomic weapons on Japan, praise for the leadership and power that had brought America through gave way to a worldwide rejection of those virtues. Postwar disarmament included a lot of changes in the ways Americans saw themselves. From powerful victors we became imperialists and bullies, Big Bomb Bullies who had the power to destroy the world, not to mention anyone who happened to get in our way.

Never before had there been such an awesome arsenal in one nation. So awesome that other nations sought out ways to paralyze that power without risking a self-destructive confrontation. The most massive and concentrated effort in the history of leveling (a kind of international Manhattan Project of passive violence) undermined America with guilt and overloaded her with responsibility.

What never could have been taken from us after World War II we gave away. We felt dangerous and lonely at the top and looked for the safety and security of "friends," and, of course, the markets those friends could offer. We accepted the responsibility for rebuilding the world, not in the spirit of international community but out of a strong sense of guilt. Somehow our strength and ability to survive made us responsible for the destruction, as if we had been the victorious aggressor in a world of innocent victims. We had, in our display of active and potential power, crossed the line between hero and monster. Our "allies" were like Richard Pryor's hometown friends: "You ain't shit. Lemme have a dollar. . . ."

In the eyes of the world and her own people America was a giant. But a stooping giant. Her citizens accepted the image of the Ugly American. We were the first people to feel victimized by victory. Gulliver was in the hands of the Lilliputians.

We resorted to manipulation rather than outright force. The "War Department" became the "Department of Defense." Opinion polls and propaganda mills sampled and shaped people like assembly line chocolates. Containment became our idea, containment of power. *Not* using the power available to a nation or an individual was a new idea. But then, never before could a weapon so completely destroy its creator. Our power made us vulnerable. We were the victimizers and the victimized all at once.

In our confusion as we tried to play down our image as a genocidal maniac and an ugly giant, while pushing to maintain covert control over changing world politics and economics, we developed as a nation and a people into Violent Sheep. The desire for military supremacy that motivated America and every other country up to the moment the bomb was dropped over Hiroshima many saw as no longer rational. The generation gap Margaret Mead spoke of opened in that instant.

As nations accepted the new limitations and rules of the cold war, people began to incorporate these attitudes into the way they saw themselves. Denying power became fashionable. It could be used as strategically and effectively in personal relationships as in global politics. (Coincidentally, the tranquilizer was introduced to America just at the time that our national character de-emphasized "big stick" diplomacy in favor of the virtues of pacification.)

Though some members of the pre-bomb generation still wanted America to take its "ordained" place as the world's leader, the postwar personality was less interested in leadership than in personal survival and material comforts. The "crisis of leadership" that was so often expressed in the 1970's has its roots in this cold war adaptation to the leveling of power. Being an enthusiastic, visible leader was a foolish and burdensome business, and young people were looking for less dangerous and less ostentatious ways to be powerful.

Even a communist worker, who once would have been praised and honored for his achievement in production, now suffers the effects of leveling. Leveling is global. It crosses all ideologies.

According to *Izvestia*, Gennady Bogomolov "is not the pride and joy of his plant's managers or party officials," even though he turns out ten times more parts from his milling machine in a Leningrad factory than the average worker. They have accused him of "being vain and seeking glory," have hounded him to slow down, have set special standards for him alone (three to five times the average), and have implied that he cheated by working weekends.

Most people working in group efforts are leveled. There's a pejorative word that describes those who do more than is required of them: "overachiever."

Although the pay was low, a friend of mine chose to work at a treatment center for the mentally retarded. She left a high-paying job because it no longer challenged her. The intangible rewards she found in using her special skill with people were worth the pay cut. After a few weeks spent observing the routine of the center, she was assigned a case load and began to get to know her patients. She worked long hours, often spending her free time with some particularly difficult patients, whose severe retardation had caused everyone else to give up on them and provide them only the barest custodial care.

She was just making headway with one woman when her

supervisor summoned her into his office. He told her that though the center was happy that she had so much time to work with the patients, it was not a good idea for anyone to work "unauthorized overtime," even if this time was volunteered. Since she thought it was a *very good* idea, she continued her concentrated efforts with extraordinary results.

The next time she was called in, her supervisor was not as pleasant or subtle. She was told her special efforts were creating dissension among her co-workers and that the center's policy dictated the precise hours a staff member could work.

She argued with him. She defended her overtime work by pointing out the obvious progress she had made with the difficult patients. But the supervisor said that was irrelevant. Stunned that he didn't care about the patients' progress, she announced that she was going to continue to work with the patients the best way she knew how. Her supervisor answered that if that included working overtime she would be fired.

Two days later she was fired. Despite her devotion and her apparent progress (all of which was used to make a case against her) she was "terminated" for being "disruptive."

The punishment for violating leveling agreements by taking initiative is expulsion and ostracism from the group, the same group that claims to revere personal initiative. Ostracism has always been a powerful weapon. In our society of already isolated and alienated people (who were trained as much by peer pressure as by their parents), ostracism is more powerful than ever. The threat of this weapon explains why so many people are satisfied—even eager—to be "just normal" like everyone else.

I've known teachers who were forced to eat alone in the teachers' lunchroom because they were spending extra time tutoring students after school. And I've known policemen who were shut out of their precinct fraternity because they taught sports to slum kids on their off hours. Someone even told me about a neighbor of his who was ostracized by everyone on the block when he had his gardener lay out a whole "prefab" lawn while everyone else was struggling with seeds and fertilizer.

"What he does is his business," my informant explained, "but he doesn't have to be so ostentatious."

The seeds of the women's movement have their roots in protest against leveling. But as soon as the movement was established it had to face its own leveling. Filmmaker Shirley Clarke, ignored by the movement, wrote, "Women who were already successful were not invited to participate. To this day I rarely receive literature. They thought we were traitors who had compromised ourselves in becoming successful. That wasn't so. Mostly we were quite lonely."

Leveling is not necessarily obvious or dramatic. It is most often an everyday pressure that is overlooked or passively accepted. The leveling we do to ourselves is almost invisible. *Self-leveling* anticipates the leveling of the group, much as a small child slaps her own hands for breaking some household rule unobserved. Women are most obvious in their self-leveling, a reaction to being put down for rising above their expected level that will take years to overcome.

The woman on the other end of the phone had been to several of my larger dinner parties. In the middle of our conversation she apologized for not inviting me to her house for dinner.

"I'd love to have you over for dinner, but I don't cook much."

"So what? That's okay."

"Well, it's not just that I don't cook much. It's, well, *you* have such feasts."

"I don't have *feasts*."

"C'mon, you're really a gourmet cook. I mean, not like me. I just cook regular, simple, healthy meals."

"What's wrong with simple meals?"

"You think you'd mind eating just a simple meal?"

"Of course I wouldn't mind. Look, I've been cooking since I was a kid. I enjoy cooking, but when I'm invited to someone's house the meal's not important. Getting together with people is what counts. Who cares if they order in a pizza?"

"You really don't think the meal's that important?"

"Naw, not important at all."

I leveled myself. I've spent many hours preparing the "feasts" this woman mentioned. It was important to me that the food I served was not just OK but great, yet I told this woman that meals weren't important, putting down all my work to make her feel comfortable. She and I could now be on the same level. My next "feast" would be no better than her order-in pizza. She could invite me to dinner now.

Jane O'Reilly wrote in *Vogue* magazine:

> Yesterday, I staggered around the corner in a supermarket and pushed my cart directly into another woman's foot. Before I could gasp, before I could spring forward with a crumpled Kleenex to staunch the wound, even before I could finish rolling the cart off her foot, she spoke.
> "I'm sorry," she said.
> "Why are you sorry?" I asked, as I patted her ankle with my Kleenex.
> She said, "I should have seen you coming. I shouldn't have been in the middle of the aisle. Oh, I'm terribly sorry. I usually carry a band-aid in my purse, but I didn't today." She limped off down the aisle muttering, "I'm sorry. I'm sorry."
> She had utterly defeated me in the *mea culpa* competition.

Writer Diane Broughton doesn't want to be in a *mea culpa* competition but ends up in one anyway:

> Even when they've made it, there are people around who keep them from knowing it, people who devote their lives to keeping a writer from getting uppity. It can be a producer, an editor, or a relative. But it isn't just writers who never get the feel of the brass ring. I wonder how many other people described as "successful" break into laughter when they read that word applied to them.

As Broughton tells how success, or the sound of it, prevented a reunion between her and an old friend, I could feel the pressure of leveling. A friend was "scared off" by Broughton's "rattling off my credits," trying to prove that she was "someone worthy of having a cup of coffee with." Instead of being able to revel in her accomplishments with her old friend, Broughton was forced to realize that the only way she could remain friendly with her was to become a self-leveler.

It might have been this malignant contaminating idea of "success" that prevented two old friends from breaking bread together, and it probably isn't the first time. So, to old friends who might want to contact me but are put off by this "successful writer" thing, let me say this: it's not true. I can match my poverty, anonymity, and insecurity against anyone's. I'm a comfort to be around.

The most basic compromise of one's integrity lies in the urge to "give it all up" to suit someone else's needs, to give talent away in order to comfort the untalented. Leveling does this. It's a passively violent tactic that keeps people from flourishing, turns leadership into glorified slavery, and forces (in a world that can blow itself up) the political ideal of "containment of power" on nations of people who already feel powerless.

While leveling reduces and controls *people*, another effective technique bends and shapes *ideas*, making them into covert weapons and using them as convenient shelters. As someone once said, "Ideas are not responsible for the people who follow them." The Flock's successful leveling and warping of ideas accounts for much of the unseen and unchecked passive violence many people accept and use in our new society.

Idea Warping

Things are seldom what they seem.
Skim milk masquerades as cream.
W.S. Gilbert, *H.M.S. Pinafore*

Mean? What does it mean?
It means precisely what I want it to mean,
neither more nor less.
Lewis Carroll, *Alice In Wonderland*

What semantics tells us happens to words also happens to ideas: Their meanings change by common usage to fit existing needs. When some important or popular idea is used as the source or justification for behavior that really has nothing to do with the original idea (and may actually conflict with it), the idea can be considered "warped." The use of idea warps to mask violence—to make it seem like something else or to justify it—is a basic tactic of the passively violent.

"To thine own self be true" has been warped from a prescription for personal integrity to a justification for selfishness. It has allowed the most reprehensible actions to be made into splendid achievements. It has been translated into popular books and philosophies that prize manipulation, victimization, and "looking out for number one."

An idea may have reached its ultimate expression or it may be in the process of change. It could be sitting anywhere on a continuum from what it orginally expressed to what it will finally become. Like the early theoreticians in atomic energy, we can only speculate about the result.

In a television documentary about families, a mother sends her little boy to his room. He has been running around the kitchen while she is trying to make dinner. Her reaction is a stunning example of idea warped Transcendental Meditation.

"Don't you think it's time for you to go to your room," she says loudly through clenched teeth, "and meditate?"

There are many popular and well-intentioned ideas that

119

are on my list of all-time favorite idea warps. Here are some short examples with brief comments and idea warped translations:

The meek shall inherit the earth.

A "golden oldie" idea warp, it has been used to justify and even glorify passivity. Nowhere does it limit what the meek may do while they're waiting for their inheritance. It has been politically twisted to mean the *dictatorship of the proletariat*.

Christ died for our sins.

He's our surrogate, so we are not ultimately responsible. Since he's already dead and nothing is said about his dying for our three, ten, or seven hundred sins, the flexibility of the proclamation leaves us with infinite possibilities for transgression. Absolution is just around the corner.

All men are created equal.

No one is better than anyone else, no matter what. This leaves a lot of room for the leveling of leaders, geniuses, and other deviants who may think that just because they're contributing more they have a right to special considerations.

Idea warps can be dangerous, not just because they can screen passive violence but because their cumulative effect can create open violence and disorder.

The "war" on poverty and the welfare system are classic idea warps. Welfare has its roots in biblical decree. Hebrews 13:16 presents the divine idea of charity in its original simplicity: "To do good and to distribute, forget not; for with such sacrifices God is well pleased." Charity is now a top-heavy business with government officials and bureaucrats its prime beneficiaries. I doubt whether God is well pleased with the gigantic impersonal structure that now administers America's health, education, and welfare. Its overloaded workers see themselves as greater victims of this complicated system than the people they are supposed to help. The taxpayers who support this destructive and cumbersome system feel similarly victimized. What was a holy responsibility has become a terrible secular burden.

The difference between what is and what is said to be is a breeding ground for rage, cynicism, and nihilism.

The concept of pacifism has been warped to mask violence and the assumption of power. Its original intent was clear and absolute. It was sensitively articulated in early Taoist writings going back to Lao-tzu in the sixth century B.C. Pacifism appeared again in Buddhism and Hinduism and then in early Christianity. Most recently the idea was eloquently represented by Gandhi and Martin Luther King. Gandhi based his nonviolence on the Hindu *Bhagavad-Gita* and the Christian New Testament.

"*Ahimsa* (nonviolence)," he wrote, "is not merely a negative state of harmlessness but it is a positive state of love, of doing good even to the evildoer."

When Gandhi wrote the following, he opened the way for nonviolence to be twisted into a justification for violence: "It [nonviolence] does not mean helping the evildoer to continue to wrong or tolerating it by passive acquiescence. On the contrary, love, the active state of *Ahimsa,* requires you to resist the wrongdoer by dissociating yourself from him even though it may offend him or injure him physically."

Gandhi intends to make it clear that nonviolence should not imply complicity with evil and that *dissociation* is essential. Somehow the mandate that permitted that dissociation "even though it may offend or injure him physically" became dovetailed with Marxist and other revolutionary principles in the 1960s and became a pacifist manifesto for provoking violence—a complete warp of Gandhian principles.

The ideology of pacifism, with all its religious and political implications, was warped into an everyday tactic to accommodate passively violent personalities, warped from the nonviolent direct action of Gandhi and Martin Luther King to passively violent indirect action by everyone who felt disenfranchised.

Black demonstrators protesting segregation in the South of the late 1950s evolved a disciplined strategy of "going limp" and not fighting back against violently racist counterdemonstrators. It was a difficult but practical tactic, initiated by Dr. King and developed by other nonviolent protest groups to be used in their

highly effective sit-ins. But whereas the pacifism and nonviolence of the unarmed and disenfranchised was a rational and
effective political tactic to achieve racial justice, it was warped by
many white middle-class rebels who were looking for a way to
express their disenchantment and boredom. The open assertion
of power had become repugnant to postwar middle-class young
people, bred in the politics of guilt and containment. Many of
them warped pacificism and its nonviolent principles to provoke
angry reactionaries—to show the world what the opposition
really was and to give the radicals a sense of moral superiority.
What had been philosophically adopted as a means of liberation
from violence became a means of provoking violence.

"Scratch a nation of cheaters," someone wrote in a letter to the
Los Angeles Times, "and you will find a nation of victims, at least
a nation of citizens who are taught at almost every turn that they
are victims. In our society, more than in any other recently, the
major urge has been to make us feel that we are all victims
(except for a few, carefully selected victimizers). This is the very
nature of reform and liberation movements. . . ."

A member of British Parliament, W. J. Brown, tells how this
"very nature" evolves, how we get from reform and liberation to
cheating:

> The idea, the inspiration, originates in the internal world, the
> world of spirit. But just as human spirit must incarnate in a
> body, so must the idea incarnate in an organization. Whether
> the organization be political, religious or social is immaterial.
> . . . The point is that, the idea having embodied itself in an
> organization, the organization then proceeds to slay the idea
> which gave it birth.

Playwright Eugene Ionesco reacts to the warp he found in the
idea of "death with dignity":

> Only yesterday we did our best to keep up the spirits of a
> terminally ill patient. But today a new approach is taking shape:
> We cannot evade the issue of dying, but it should be death with

dignity. How considerate! The entire propaganda, the whole temper of our times, is based on lies and deceit; every truth gets twisted around, nothing is cast in its true light, we are living a lie. . . .

But now the white lies that kept hope alive in terminally ill patients are considered inexcusable. And all this in the name of "human dignity," which at other times we mock and spit upon.

Much passive violence has been inflicted under the banner of human dignity. The recent movement for children's liberation arose because some people realized that children were being mistreated by a system of laws originally designed to protect them. Children were being locked up for offenses that would not be illegal if they were adults—offenses like truancy and "incorrigibility"—and the places they were locked up in were found to add to whatever problems the children may have already had. So, after a lot of heated debate, many of those oppressive laws were repealed. The result has been that, rather than being badly cared for, most children in trouble have ceased to be cared for at all. Policemen have decided not to bother to pick up runaways, many of whom were being physically and sexually exploited, since the officers thought it would be futile to try to hold them.

The idea of children's liberation was fine, but actualizing the idea brought serious problems. The laws that were passed to give children added supports from society became warped to allow children to be neglected and mistreated. Then, in order for them to be "liberated" from this mistreatment, other laws were repealed, allowing a new violence, with a depersonalized and much less obvious oppressor.

Both "death with dignity" and the movement for children's liberation coincide with a time when people are looking for ways to *avoid* responsibility, personal entanglements, and commitments. Each warp of these humanistic ideas allows people to excuse their abandonment of hopeless cases, children and the dying among them, behind the rhetoric of Truth, Freedom, and Dignity.

"Form follows function" was Louis Henri Sullivan's architectural axiom. Psychologically, form (*philosophies*) also follows function (*personalities*).

When A. S. Neill first wrote about his school in England called Summerhill, not too many people paid attention. Summerhill was Neill's expression of love and faith in the young, a personal creation of the warm and caring family every child wants and needs. He called it a school, and, in the broadest sense, it was. But the things children learned there were more important than the courses in any academically and socially more prestigious academy. They learned responsibility and trust and were taught how to find answers to their personal and educational questions.

The idea that Neill transmitted in his book, *Summerhill*, was that freedom helped children learn. He found this freedom essential for children to develop their skills and capacities for cooperative effort. When the arguments for "freedom" began their crescendo in the early sixties, Neill's book became the bible of educational reform. It also gave people a different way of dealing with children that seemed to fit the emerging way of living.

But the American "alternative schools" that espoused Neill's philosophy were very different from Summerhill. Neill understood that for a school to provide real freedom for children it had to have strong and capable adult leaders (like himself). The "total" freedom of his school that both shocked and excited most readers and visitors could only exist under special conditions. In order for children to run free, the adults around them had to have less freedom themselves. They had to be more disciplined than teachers in a conventional school. Children could run free only if there were adults around them who could deal with their crises, fights, injuries, and dangers.

The young adults who flocked to "teach" in schools of the Summerhill type were looking for a place for their *own* freedom. Feeling neither strong nor capable (or very adult), they were looking for "family," for an A. S. Neill daddy, and for a place where they would be free of expectations and responsibilities. They identified with the children, whom they saw as victims of the "system." The line between themselves and the children they were to teach disappeared, and they saw themselves and the children as one. The idea of Summerhill became their hiding place, their attempt at finding freedom in the guise of providing it.

The American Summerhill movement failed. And A. S. Neill, just before his death, wrote a sequel to his first book. It was called *Freedom, Not License*.

It is the business of social critics, economists, and journalists to watch ideas, to see how they're being warped, and maybe even to predict where particular warps will take us. The following report illustrates an idea warp from its historical root to its violent turn. The idea under the magnifying glass here is the "right to treatment," liberating people from the violence of the locked wards of mental institutions.

Peter Koenig, writing in *The New York Times Magazine*, reports on the "dumping" of mental patients in rundown hotels: "Dumping dates back to the fifties, to the invention of tranquilizers, and to the subsequent ascendance of a medical ideology rooted in the axiom that disturbed patients are better off close to home than locked away out of sight."

Good idea. Anyone would agree offhand that harmless people are better off "close to home" than they are locked away in a "snake pit."

But the healthy possibilities suggested by the patients' being "close to home" were soon superseded by movements that justified actions at least as cruel as those in the hospitals from which many patients would soon be "liberated." The new violence was, in a way, even crueller, because it was less easily identifiable.

Koenig explains the idea warp. The idea that "close to home" was better than "locked away out of sight" led to the dumping of thousands of mentally ill, totally isolated and vulnerable, into cheap hotels and big city streets.

Syncopate this [the "close to home" idea] with the civil rights movement, which eventually extended its concern to the mentally ill, and Supreme Court rulings such as the one handed down in 1975, declaring that states cannot constitutionally detain *without treatment* [italics added] "a non-dangerous individual who is capable of surviving safely in freedom by himself or with the help of willing and responsible family members and friends," and one begins to understand how and why we are now dumping the mentally ill out of hospitals instead of into them. In 1955, there were 550,000 patients in state mental hospitals across the country; today, there are 190,000.

The possibility of improved treatment for these "non-dangerous" sick people was not a serious consideration, not when the mental health establishment could get as much money or more for "monitoring" them outside without having to worry about "treatment." If many people had had "willing and responsible family members and friends," they wouldn't have ended up in the hospital in the first place. And very few of them found such friends in the cold and dangerous slum hotels they were dumped into.

The violence here was even more insidious than the institutional variety, since the active victimizers were no longer identifiable. The new, passively violent "monitoring" organization was safely out of sight.

Teacher and author Alan Cliburn reports a conversation he had with a friend, a high school teacher who had just taught summer school in one of the country's largest school districts.

He liked the experience—and the additional paycheck—and wants to do it again. To assure this, he failed no one in either of his two classes.

"You mean no one deserved a failing mark?" I questioned, unable to believe it.

"Well, there was this one kid who had around fourteen points out of a possible one hundred fifty," he admitted. "But he was a nice kid who came every day and never gave me any trouble."

"Yeah, but if he only had fourteen points," I began.

"Look, if I had failed him, he would've had to repeat the class—again—and he wouldn't have gotten anything out of it that time, either," came the reply. "I'm saving the taxpayers some money and giving the kid a break, too."

The subject my friend teaches, incidentally, is English.

He also told me about another kid who was borderline between a "C" and a "D," but who "just couldn't make it" the day of the final, therefore putting his point total into the "D" category.

"He got a 'C,' " my friend said. "He plays football. He needed a 'C' to make the team this fall."

"Yeah, but—"

"Besides, he used pretty good logic when he came in to talk to me about it," my friend continued. "He asked me what I was giving this other kid, the boy with fourteen points. When I told him a 'D,' he reminded me that he had done a lot more work than that guy and certainly deserved a better grade. I had to agree."

"Except that the other guy really deserves an 'F'!" I exclaimed.

"You don't understand the system," he informed me rather simply.

The warp in this teacher's role "to educate" is clarified by a report released by the U. S. Office of Education. It stated that more than twenty-three million American adults, one in every five, were too ignorant to function effectively in society.

"It is surprising, perhaps even shocking," the report said, "to suggest that approximately one of five Americans is incompetent or functions with difficulty and that about half of the adult population is merely functional and not at all proficient in necessary skills and knowledges."

The researchers said they had found the situation more dismal than believed previously: "Thirty-nine million were 'functional but not proficient' in such tests as reading a newspaper grocery ad."

The project director at the University of Texas, who received one million dollars to conduct the study, left us with a million dollar warp when he speculated: "Educators do a reasonably good job of preparing students for more education, but perhaps not as good a job in preparing students for life."

What happens to people left with twelve years of schooling and no education? If it is true that the gap between what is and what is said to be breeds rage, cynicism, and nihilism, we have an answer that will be as socially devastating as any future superwar.

The beginning symptoms of that rage are already with us: more students dropping out of school, more violence in them. American schools are now spending as much on vandalism as on new textbooks. No matter how hard people try not to understand it, this destruction is not without a message.

The summation of the Texas study is particularly important for understanding the violence of the educationally neglected and abandoned:

> As long as "literacy" is conceived to be nothing more than the ability to read and write one's name . . . then the United States does not have a significant problem.
>
> On the other hand, if the concern is with the adult who does not possess those skills and knowledges which are requisites to adult competence, then the results of the research suggest that there is, indeed, a widespread discrepancy in our adult population between what is required of them and what they achieve.

The idea of education for all Americans was realized to give even the most disenfranchised a better chance at the American dream. But the idea became warped by an organization that became the "educational establishment," whose hunger for survival didn't necessarily include the survival of its students.

I don't know how many good ideas have been warped to violent conclusions, maybe all of them in some way and by someone. The danger of idea warping is not just that ideas get changed but that they may be changed toward violent ends. It is in the nature of passively violent people to seek out worthwhile and socially acceptable ideas and use them as justification and cover for aggression. Probably every major religious, philosophical, political, or psychological idea has been distorted to hurt someone.

Idea warps affect not only the way we see peace, dying, children, illness, and education, the major issues of life, but also the way we see ourselves. Ideas warped for our own improvement mask a lot of violence between us and the people we're closest to.

The passing parade of fad therapies allows for the illusion of personal growth and change, often while covering a passively violent determination to control others. People use philosophical banners to justify their behavior.

The flurry of interest in "assertiveness training" that began in the mid-seventies seemed at first glance a good idea for people who needed a way out of self-destructive passivity. It presented them with an effective way to deal with the world. But as I read the books and talked to people who were using this training, I felt that this idea, which was meant to train passive people, was being used by passively violent people to make their passive violence more effective.

"What's the difference between assertiveness and aggression?" I asked a therapist acquaintance of mine.

"It's a difference in control," she explained.

"You mean a difference in the way one person controls another?" I asked, somewhat shocked at the openness of the intended violence.

"Oh, no," she was quick to point out, "not *that* kind of control. I'm talking about self-control. The assertive person has himself under control, whereas the aggressive person has lost control. It's really a matter of effectiveness and how a person feels about himself."

"I can't see the difference as far as the person on the other end of the relationship is concerned," I replied. "The goals seem to be the same. Only the style or approach is different. What about the person who's acted *upon*? How does he tell the difference?"

"Our emphasis is not on that person," she admitted. "What we're trying to do is to get people to express their wishes more effectively."

"Then there's no real difference between assertive or aggressive if you're looking at it from the getting end."

"We're concerned about what our patients need to do for *themselves*," she emphasized again.

"Yeah, OK, I understand that. But the 'selves' that the training is addressing itself to live in a context of other people." I began to feel a little aggressive.

"Yes, that's true," she asserted. "And they aren't dealing

effectively with those other people. We can't deal with the other people but we can help our patients to assert themselves with those people. Passive people have a problem with this."

As our conversation went around in circles, she became more "assertive" and my reaction became more "aggressive." It was perfect.

After the conversation I went back to my books and articles on assertiveness training. "You can disarm insistent trouble seekers," one article explained, "with a cheerful smile instead of a counterattack, because *it leaves them feeling at a loss.* [Italics added.] Try an inquiring, expectant look that says without words: 'And what else?' You can also greet their opening thrust with 'I see,' saying, 'You know, I really don't understand. Could you put that more clearly?' "

This is not a lesson to bring the passive victim out into the world with some sense of self. This is training in psychological guerilla warfare and is every bit as violent as a punch in the mouth. But by idea-warped definition, it somehow escapes the stigma of aggression.

Another treatise on assertiveness does acknowledge open aggression, and the manipulative motive of the training: "Fighting, verbal or otherwise, undoubtedly stimulates a lot of people and may do them some good. If it makes you feel better and stronger, the only question is whether you can afford it. You can safely go at some people, but what about a supervisor, a prospective customer or *someone you have to get along with* [italics added] and who resents argumentative attitudes?"

This training bears watching. It preaches safe, disarming violence behind a warped idea of non-aggression. It attempts to give psychological violence the legitimacy of a rational code of protective behavior. It outlines offensive tactics in defensive terms.

Assertiveness training is a good idea. It's the warp that makes it dangerous. Most other therapies have been abused in the same way. Born Again, Scientology, behavior modification, psychoanalysis, macrobiotics are all programs that offer positive approaches to life. And all are warped by many of their transient followers to justify personal imperialism. In expanding their own "space" the followers intrude on the boundaries of others.

Too many therapies make us easy marks for authoritarian social control. They teach us to control internal states, our own and those of people around us, while denying responsibility for injustice, cruelty, and suffering. They focus on the inferiority complex instead of the military-industrial complex, body movements instead of social movements, the abstract possibilities of the future instead of the concrete responsibilities of the present. Though people live in both an internal and an external world, the movement toward psychological awareness has made self-concern and social involvement mutually exclusive.

Psychologist James A. Dyal explains the potential for passive control that lies in idea-warped "therapies": "The Machiavellian hell of the twenty-first century is not likely to be engineered by Big Brother's bad henchmen, but by a mild-looking group of therapists who, like the Grand Inquisitor, would be doing what they did to help you."

Whether the engineers of that "Machiavellian hell" are therapists or other unelected decision makers, one thing is certain. They will control people and events even more effectively and with greater protection than their twentieth century prototypes unless their existence and methods are exposed and challenged.

The Expertocracy:
Little Lost Shepherds

Our weather forecasters say the low
tonight will be 48°. The temperature
now in downtown L.A. is 42°.
    DJ on Los Angeles radio station

It seems that the same people are always advising us, in and out of wars, up and down the economic ladder, and around the most pressing environmental, moral, and social issues. Although their advice has been as often bad as good, their prestige and power are secure. They are more secure than the people who are elected or anointed to lead. They are not vulnerable or often even visible, but their control of power appears to be steady and increasing.

These platoons of experts, advisors, consultants, professionals, thinkers, and predictors are the expertocracy. Born out of the marriage of bureaucracy and university-trained pragmatism, they live without conscience or concern for the effects of their recommendations. By selling questionable skills, breakable promises, false security, and inaccurate predictions they create disappointment and rage. Their violence lies in the discrepancy between what they can do and what they promise.

The same people who advised us to fight the Korean and Vietnamese wars, support the invasion of the Bay of Pigs, and finance the overthrow of the elected government of Chile are still counseling this government about affairs of state. And the same people who brought us one hundred percent inflation in only ten years, gas at a dollar a gallon, the removal of silver from our coins (and from behind our dollars), and the decline of American currency in the world market are still shaping our economic policies.

The people who told us that X-rays, DES, DDT, nuclear power plants and waste dumps, asbestos ceilings, and food coloring were safe are still our government's official science advisors and regulatory agency commissioners.

132

And the people who have failed to educate millions of children to read and write well enough to be employable are the same people advising us to spend billions of dollars on more of the same failure.

In order to compete with their rivals, political leaders create an atmosphere of passive violence by mouthing impossible commitments, as their advisors have told them to do. Their followers have unrealistic expectations, which lead them to be disappointed and frustrated. At the same time the advisors use the anonymity and protection that the leaders offer them to establish a covert and secure power base. Such basic considerations as truth, justice, or excellence are not important in the relationship between leader and expert. Both are involved in a pragmatic struggle for power. The leader's struggle is visible to the public; the expert's struggle is not. The expert usually survives the leader.

In America, the expert benefits from a symbiotic relationship with power, and, in the long run, acquires more of it than the transients who are elected to office. (In other countries with more violent paths to power, the experts often share the grim fate of their deposed benefactors—one slight compensation for having totalitarian rule.) Adding to the expert's longevity is the fact that the leader who anoints him must protect him to keep up his own image as a competent decision maker. Even if the experts are absolutely wrong, few leaders can admit having made a mistake by using them in the first place. So experts are passed on in much the same way that many people would pass on counterfeit money rather than be penalized for unknowingly accepting it. Experts become more powerful than accountable, a situation which usually means trouble.

The leader-expert relationship is unique. The line between servant and master, passive and dominant, shifts often and sometimes disappears completely. To paraphrase the end of an old limerick, it is at times impossible to tell who is doing what and with which and to whom.

The shift of responsibility and power back and forth between the leader and his advisors has become an active political shell game. Leaders use advisors to diffuse their responsibility for decisions of war and foreign policy and for establishing priorities and policies for domestic affairs. By doing this, leaders now say, however implicitly, "I was only following advice," a significant variation of the cliché formerly reserved for subordinates who announced, "I was only following orders."

Though the leader is responsible for choosing his experts, he nonetheless uses them to dodge responsibility for unpopular decisions. This maneuver provides leaders with a faceless scapegoat whenever their own effectiveness or ability is challenged. (Experts whose faces are known give up some of their immunity, a slight risk and inconvenience that they can usually hand down to anonymous subordinates.)

In the meantime, experts use the protected and privileged position provided by the leader to establish their own control over leaders and events. Despite the periodic need to blame the expert (an action that usually has no long-lasting impact), expertise is both valued and feared by leaders, who are vulnerable to its accumulated power. The advisor with expertocratic inclinations is able to turn this vulnerability and fear to his own advantage. In this way the expert rises to invisible positions of power. Ideally he has maximum covert power with minimum vulnerability, status with safety. This arrangement also assures future generations of poor leaders and experts.

The failure of the expertocracy is not a new phenomenon. Let us not forget the Edsel, the Titanic, the Maginot Line, and Pearl Harbor. The CIA, FBI, and State Department have given presidents wrong advice for so long and so often that Watergates, domestic surveillances, and coverups don't meet as much with public shock or outrage as with passive and resigned disgust. Not surprisingly, people are no more capable than their leaders of resisting expertocratic violence.

Simply by establishing oneself as a lawyer, doctor, social worker, educator, biologist, city planner, economist, journalist, psychologist, engineer, physicist, or political scientist one assumes a mantle of authority. Once that authority is accepted or validated by an organization it carries with it the ability to injure people while disarming their ability to retaliate. The social importance of degrees, diplomas, and memberships in professional associations comes from people's fear of resisting established authority and education, which conditions them to submit to it. The expertocrat depends on this submissiveness to keep and increase his power.

I should make it clear that there are experts who are not expertocrats. Expertise may be objectively defined by an absolute standard of knowledge, or more subjectively, by a generally accepted standard. But as knowledge doesn't automatically create an expert, the expert does not automatically take the path to expertocracy. The difference lies in the responsibility each shows in his privileged position. The expert will use his power for social or scientific good, whereas the expertocrat is interested primarily in expanding his personal power while keeping his security. The expertocrat finds easy rationalizations for denying social responsibility in the ignorance or ingratitude of the public. The expert may feel the burden of his responsibility but is essentially an optimist. The expertocrat uses the frustration and violence he sees around him to indulge in immobilizing cynicism. He has feet of clay, like everyone else. He may have been trained to find answers, but he can't be expected to know *everything*. He meets criticism by proclaiming his impotence.

The expertocrat has used his expertise as the means to his ends—title and position and influence. He is preoccupied with his position in his organization and may twist facts to keep it. The expert is concerned with the integrity of his work, even risking the disfavor of his organization.

Even when the expert's ideas are warped by others into vehicles for overt or passive violence, he remains accountable for them and will inform the public about potential abuses. Einstein did this with the results of his work in atomic fission and its application to nuclear bombs. He was an expert concerned with the unintended side effects of his work.

There is a direct link between social workers, police, caseworkers, probation officials, and judges (among others) and the poor people who commit violence. These experts, who have earned degrees to learn what to do about social problems, often claim to be greater victims of the "system" than the clients or culprits they face every day.

"Within the bureaucracy I have no power," some say.

"My training hasn't prepared me for this," cry others.

"My caseload is so great I can't do decent work with anyone," say most of them.

But if expertocrats are helpless to get things done, they insist on their rewards: money, security, tenure. Poor people must accept a dismaying fact. The person they depend on for their health, education, and welfare is himself overwhelmed by the demands made on him. Yet his importance guarantees his right to be paid for what he does. Many social service recipients can't reconcile themselves to someone making what seems to be a lot of money for the privilege of being more victimized by the system than they are.

The poor, the young, and the old have come to know the social service expertocracy for the sham that it is. People have always known about corruption, but being paid to be helpless is a new wrinkle that creates a lot of confusion, frustration, and anger.

The violence underlying the helplessness of the expertocrat lies in a double-edged awareness: "I *need* this dude who says *he's* helpless," and "If he's so damned helpless, how come he's getting paid for it?"

The passive violence of the expertocracy foments active violence in the population at large. Problems have become commodities, sold by experts, complete with impersonal statistics and incomprehensible recommendations, to visible, recognizable leaders.

People have stopped believing that the study of social problems precedes solutions. They know that the study of problems is an end in itself and this realization creates its own violent desperation.

Sam Brown, director of the government's VISTA and Peace Corps programs, understands people's frustration with the expertocracy. "For over forty years," says Brown, "we have invested our money and our hopes in creating government institutions and federal programs to realize our dream of a just society. Now those dreams have become a bureaucratic nightmare, creating massive anonymous programs which provide visible benefits only to social planners and government bureaucrats."

But of course, the "bureaucracy" is only the working class of the expertocracy. The social planners, the experts, are the elite, the ones whose "dreams have become a . . . nightmare." The bureaucracy is cumbersome and violent, one of the many nightmares created by social architects. The damage wrought by the maze of bureaus and their maddening procedures may be unsurpassed even in the history of warfare. But though bureaucracies are creations of expertocratic malfeasance, the experts have managed to remain aloof from most of the public outrage created by their bureaucratic offspring.

I don't want to minimize the violent effect of bureaucracies. Stories are common of tortuous attempts to make them work or even to communicate with them on the most essential levels. They contribute to the daily violence in our lives. But I think it is important to make a distinction. There is the bureaucracy, the "ten-ton marshmallow," with its bureaucrats, commonly referred to as "headless nails—once they're in you can never get them out." Then there are the expertocrats, behind-the-scenes instigators of bureaucratic violence. The bureaucracy is the madhouse and bureaucrats are the keepers, the guards, the hired guns. The experts conceive the institutions and they seduce an uninformed leadership into accepting the actual nuts and bolts and contracts.

The tandem violence of the experts and their hired hands is the violence that comes from violation and intrusion, from the excesses of misrepresentation. People are more aware than ever that the institutions and procedures intended to protect and serve them have become abusive, stagnant, and counterproductive.

Citizens know that many teachers have gone to college to become teachers, not to teach children; that many people become social workers for reasons irrelevant to social work. They know that doctors may be more concerned with status and money than with treating the sick; that lawyers often follow their profession for other reasons than to battle with legal inequities. So while expertocrats sew themselves even more tightly into the protective covers of professional associations and binding agreements, average people are coming to have less and less faith in expertise.

Professional associations that once offered some comfort and security to laymen have been unmasked as nothing more than additional layers of insulation for professional incompetence. Once portrayed as the "check and balance" to professional lack of competence or abuse of power, professional associations have proven ineffective in ferreting out problems. In many cases they perpetuate abuse.

Recent New York State Assembly reports charged that doctors, hospitals, and medical societies in New York State have consistently evaded their responsibility to protect the public against harm from incompetent or unethical physicians. With very few exceptions, the report said, doctors do not report instances of professional misconduct to regulatory agencies and "very few appear to consider it their obligation to do so."

The report said that when medical abuses become too flagrant to disregard, colleagues help the abuser to leave quietly and set up practice elsewhere. They may even help him alter his medical records to cover up evidence of misconduct or negligence.

"Our first look at the way medicine is practiced in New York reveals a 'see no evil, hear no evil, speak no evil' attitude which pervades the profession," the report states. And though New York may be one of the few states to study this problem, we can be sure that it is unique only in its willingness to report what it found. Medical practice in every state is filled with cronyism and cover-ups. No wonder that the public has responded with mounting malpractice suits. More than anything else, I think, these represent a counterviolence resulting from unkept trust. Betrayal is a very effective personal motive for violence.

As an unelected, non-productive expertocracy assumes greater power over the lives of more and more people, the potential for violent reaction multiplies. As the violence mounts, the expertocrats become even more victimized and more justified in feeling helpless. It is a perfectly parasitic relationship, the expertocracy depending on the bureaucratic chaos it has helped create to justify its existence and even its expansion. The more problems it creates, the more experts are necessary to study, interpret, and otherwise feed from it. Experts are rewarded for failure.

It is important to understand that the violence that comes from the expert's passivity rarely attacks the expert. Medical malpractice suits are only a recent exception. Most often that violence is transferred to the exposed leaders and others left unprotected by the society, while the expertocracy searches for another round of grants, fee increases, and target populations.

Consider the implications of this report by *Los Angeles Times* writer Robert Fairbanks.

SACRAMENTO—It carries a price tag of $2 million a year and the evidence says it will not reduce youth crime.

But Mrs. Pearl S. West, the director of the California Youth Authority, wants it, and Governor Brown's director of finance, Roy M. Bell, has decided to go along.

Essentially, Mrs. West wants to put 69 more parole officers in the field. Thus, the average number of parolees assigned to each officer would drop from 50 to 37 and the officers would have more time to deal with the youths in their charge.

But Bell's own staffers reported last year that *the size of parole case loads has no effect upon parolee reversions to crime.* (Italics mine.)

Specifically, the Finance Department staffers had studied several community parole centers that the CYA had set up several years ago to show that reduced case loads could cut crime reversion rates.

But the study found that the rates were not dropping. Parolees in the smaller caseloads (some as low as 12 to 1) were reverting to crime as rapidly as those in the general 50–1 population.

(CYA statistics indicate that about two thirds of CYA parolees are convicted of some new crime within five years of their release.)

As a result, the finance staffers were ready to recommend that the parole centers be shut down and that all parolees be placed in the general parole population. The action was to save about $2 million a year because the state would no longer need those extra parole officers (69 of them) in the parole centers.

It was then that Mrs. West came up with her proposed reform: Close the centers but let her keep the parole officer positions. Thus, she could cut the average case load from 50 to 37.

A spokesman for Mrs. West contended that the program is more than merely a case load reduction.

Parole officers, he explained, will be instructed to concentrate their efforts in the period immediately after the parolee's release, when experience has shown that the parolee needs guidance most. Thus crime reversion rates should decline.

But The Times has obtained a CYA memo to Mrs. West from William C. McCord, a veteran CYA official in the San Francisco Bay Area.

According to McCord, the CYA tried the "front-loaded" approach in three projects between 1961 and 1974 and it did not work.

"None of these models was more effective than the existing parole system," he said in the memo.

But Mrs. West, a Brown appointee who took over the CYA in 1976, remained adamant and Finance Director Bell eventually went along.

"Since she really wanted to start something new, I didn't feel it would be fair to cut her back," Bell explained.

As a result, the $2 million for the 69 positions remains in the post-Proposition 13 budget that Brown signed last week.

The violence here is multilayered. If we simply look at the money, we see that two million dollars given over to the whim of an appointed official does constitute a kind of theft from the taxpayers, especially given the results of the program. The use of money in one place precludes its use somewhere else. Other programs—perhaps even ones that are effective—won't be funded. Despite the distance between people and government, the public knows there is a limit to the money available to support necessary programs. People were robbed here by the whim of the official involved, and robbery is violent.

But on another level the parolees and the parole officers were also subjected to violence in the form of violent passivity. The parolee has the obligation to meet with the parole officer for a prescribed period of time. As a rule he understands that these meetings are bureaucratic rituals. They will not actually help him achieve independence and success out of prison.

For ex-convicts to see these kinds of programs supporting greater numbers of staff people, while they themselves are often unable to find even the most menial jobs, is passively violent and provocative. Even if parolees believe that the majority of the public is unaware of the waste of bureaucratic manpower, they know the experts are aware of it. They, too, are aware of it, and they deeply resent it.

Parole officers were allowed to expand their numbers, even though experience showed that these numbers would not accomplish the desired result. In this way they were made accessories to the chicanery of the top official.

The Finance Director's innocence is touching, but his feeling that a cutback wouldn't be "fair" seems to disregard totally his responsibility to the people of his state to provide funds on merit and not on vague preferential judgments. And so a program of no consequence was forced on the taxpayer, the staff, and the parolees, none of whom had a part in deciding whether the program would continue, but all of whom shared the burden. In this way expertocratic whim and non-accountability dissipates money and manpower and aggravates frustration and resentment. As the "passive" crimes of the expertocracy are analyzed for their "hidden violence," passivity itself takes on new meaning.

Consider the expertocracy's deep involvement in the war business, now called, more euphemistically, "the defense industry." Including universities and their bureaucracies, the military-industrial-academic-bureaucratic complex now accounts for the spending of about 400 billion defense dollars a year worldwide.

According to the Stockholm International Peace Research Institute, an independent disarmament organization created by the Swedish government to study and publicize the cost of the global arms race, more than four hundred thousand research and development scientists are working for military programs. That number represents more than half of the world's graduate physicists and research and development engineers.

While the danger of the ultimate active violence is underlined by the Institute's statistics (suggesting the momentum for nuclear weapons) the director of the Institute says that the death of western civilization is more likely to come through inflation fed by defense spending.

"It's obvious to most of us that increased military spending threatens the very existence of Western society," says Frank Barnaby, the Institute's director.

"If we continue to do what we are doing, unemployment is going to be much greater because of inflation. If you look at industrial investment in the United States and compare it with the possible 50 billion dollar cost of the MX (mobile missile), you will see that a private enterprise system can't go on. You'll have to move to Draconian controls and eventually to something like the Soviet system."

So the experts have us playing a no-win game. We can win the arms race and lose our economy. Or we can lose them both. Using arguments based on the threat of one nation to another, they have created a violence that transcends national boundaries. And as nationalism becomes an economic and technological anachronism, the expertocrats reappear as multinationals.

People cannot expect loyalty from an expertocrat, no allegiance to any person, company, or country. Ann Crittenden, writing in *The New York Times*, elaborates on the apolitical American consultants.

In April, 1974, Algerian President Houari Boumedienne launched the rhetorical cold war between the developing nations and the industrial powers with a fiery speech before a special session of the United Nations. To the cheers of the delegates from the Third World, he denounced the profligate ways of the West and attributed all the poor's troubles to the higher cost of goods purchased from the developed countries.

The speech made the Algerians famous as the leaders of the anti-imperialist camp. Less well known is the fact that much of it was prepared in the heart of capitalism by a team of consultants from Arthur D. Little, Inc. of Cambridge, Mass.

"We just provided them with some facts," said William A. W. Krebs, a Little vice president who was involved in the project. "It was a research job. We gave them data on such things as world price trends or the costs of projects in the United States like the highway program. *They never asked us to make a policy statement.*" (Italics added.)

The Algerian connection is just one among many illustrating the little known but ubiquitous activities of American consulting firms in the developing world. . . .

They tell one country what its export industries should be, another how to plan its energy policy for the year 2000, and a third how to restructure its education system. While their advice is not always heeded, consultants establish close personal relationships with Socialist leaders and work intimately with right-wing dictatorships. . . .

The educational aspect of economic development work is Mr. Krebs' argument against those who would criticize Little and others for working with regimes that are authoritarian or hostile to the United States.

"Keeping other countries in ignorance is never to the national advantage," he said. "It can only be to our advantage when another government can see that an American firm is free to offer objective, unbiased advice, unconstrained by the national policies of the moment."

Aside from the obvious idea warp that allows Mr. Krebs to be righteous while compromising American interests, history contradicts his notion that "our advantage" lies in offering "objective unbiased advice." Because of this unbiased advice the United States sold scrap iron to Japan immediately before an imminent war; that scrap iron became weapons that killed American soldiers. It was this same unbiased advice that preceded the sale of millions of tons of wheat to the Russians, causing the price of bread to rise along with the general cost of living in the U.S. Meanwhile the Russians were alleged to have unloaded the wheat to Italy for a fast profit. Such advice has also led to the sale of strategically valuable computers to the Soviet Union, to the sale of American ball bearings (a sale that can only have military

ramifications), and to the compromising of American interests in
the middle east. Somewhere in all this "objectivity" is a word that
is becoming lost in the multinational smokescreen. It is a word
that implies violence to one's own people. The word, in war time,
is "treason." We are not at war. But more than half a million men
have been lost in the peace since World War II.

Clearly the nature of war is changing along with the definition
of violence. And the expertocracy will benefit from the time that
elapses before the world's population catches up with the new
realities.

According to the *Washington Post,* the prospect of a global
"information war" poses the biggest threat to the United States.
John M. Eger described the growing threat to the flow of
information and how the American expertocracy has changed
the maxim "Knowledge is power" to a more pragmatic "Information is power."

> Brazil is stationing police censors at all post offices to
> intercept incoming publications that might contain anything
> "contrary to public order or to morality." Thailand has just
> raised import duties on foreign films by 1,500%. Several
> Canadian provinces now have laws that bar transmission of
> credit data out of their borders. Colombia has claimed all the
> airspace over its territory and will try to collect rent from any
> nation that parks a communications satellite there.
>
> Throughout the world, the free flow of information is under
> fire. And because the United States is the nation where the
> communications revolution is most advanced, it is often our
> publications, our films, our credit data, and our satellites that
> are under attack.
>
> According to one Commerce Department study based on
> 1967 figures, the "information industry" accounts for 46% of
> the U.S. work force and almost half the gross national product.
>
> So the prospect of an international "information war" is a
> serious threat to American interests in an increasingly interde-
> pendent world. Yet it is a threat that three U.S. Administrations
> have found no strategy to meet. . . .
>
> Many countries imposing restrictions fear cultural inunda-

tion or annihilation. They speak of "electronic colonization" or "electronic imperialism." While we see ourselves offering the developing nations information they need to survive, they see in our technology a vast threat and unwelcome change. . . .

France's minister of Justice, Louis Joinet, put the European concern most directly in a speech to an Organization for Economic Cooperation and Development symposium . . . : "Information is power, and economic information is economic power. Information has an economic value and the ability to store and process certain types of data may well give one country political and technological advantage over other countries. This in turn may lead to a *loss of national sovereignty through supranational data flows.*" (Italics added.)

To protect their "national sovereignty" against this perceived threat, many European nations are enacting a variety of data-protection laws. Most of these laws are being passed in the name of personal privacy and individual rights.

That something as "simple" as the flow of information could be vulnerable to the danger of intrusion and control in a global information war need only be compared to our own credit and data systems to be understood. The thousands of data banks in this country and their billions of bits of information have already created a personal privacy backlash—a "civil" information war. New legislation has been passed to limit information exchange, quickly followed by even newer technological developments which instantly render the legislation outmoded.

The expertocracy shapes and controls information while voters make useless gestures of self-assertion, attempting to prevent further erosion of their money and privacy. Whatever potential for violence exists in the continued and growing use and control of information, the expertocracy will test its limits.

Nowhere is the intrusion of the expertocracy more obvious than in its ability to force the people it most oppresses to adopt its dehumanized language. Expertocrats are aware of how language shapes behavior and how jargon can obscure ignorance and hostility. Understanding the impact of words on thought and action, people have fought wars to keep or regain their freedom of language. In Quebec, the transition from bilingual education to French is seen as the most potent weapon in the nationalists' move towards succession. In Brittany, a land racially more Welsh and Irish than French, Breton terrorists have exploded over two hundred bombs in government installations since 1966. They now believe, however, that teaching the Breton language will bring them more autonomy than all their bombs. According to one prominent Breton, "Learning the Breton language is our cultural revolution now."

"Language is a class weapon," says Henry Fairlie, a British journalist living in Washington who is credited, in the latest supplement to the Oxford English Dictionary, with introducing the term "the Establishment." "And the triumph of the middle class in the past few centuries has made our language a middle-class instrument. This is why the aristocrats and the underprivileged protest." He goes on to say, "The jargon of the bureaucrat is the language of someone who does not really know what he is meant to be doing."

A good example of adopting the language of bureaucracy is shown in the numbers of poor people who, along with their own jargon, speak the tongue of the expert "grantsman," the professional hustler of government money.

I'm at a conference on juvenile justice in Des Moines. One of my fellow panelists is a Sioux Indian activist and a member of the American Indian Movement, a militant organization of native Americans. As he speaks, I realize how far the expertocrats have gone in subduing this potential threat to their status quo. He speaks like one of them, thinks in their terms. He has become one of them. Even his anger is expressed in expertocratese.

> We have a lot of Indian young people who are abusing alcohol and developing antisocial attitudes and behaviors. So we are looking for some new concept in learning to keep these young people in an educational environment. We found a privately sponsored group that puts together packets of learning materials they have tagged as exposure education.
>
> It really impressed us. I think it will allow young students a variety of exposure. This private company has gone around

showing these to the schools and if the school says, "Yes, we want the student to learn this," the company says, "No, we won't give it to you if that's the idea you have." The rules are that you expose them to it—no instruction is supposed to be given. Hopefully, somewhere in this series of packets the youth will find something he wants to do. We're going to try to implement this in Sioux City, involving the Indian culture.

This militant native American's language is indistinguishable from that of the educational consultants or the entire expertocracy of the Department of Health, Education, and Welfare. But that in itself doesn't mean this man has been neutralized. Some would say that his "education" equips him to deal more effectively with the real world.

My objection, or more precisely, my fear, is that this "education" is really a reconditioning and that people will start thinking in the terms they are forced to use to communicate with the experts. As soon as people start thinking and acting in terms of the expertocracy, they lose their position as adversaries and become coopted into it.

I can't believe that this man can deal effectively with his own people and still talk about "input," "viable programs," "meaningful alternatives," "relevant options," and "job slots," even though this jargon is necessary to communicate with "sources of funding." At some point the bureaucratic game ends and real people begin. Along with the Bretons and the French Canadians I think that the control of language ultimately controls the identities of the people who use it.

In the same way, welfare mothers speak the social-work jargon of caseloads, ADC payments, subsidies, allocations, and carry-over expenses. Survival within the welfare system demands an understanding of the process and of the language. Criminals learn the language of the courts. The problem again comes when their understanding and acceptance of the system supersedes their own feelings, their lives, and their ability to find their way out of expertocratic control. Their anger, rage, and potential for violence against the system is neutralized by a more insidious violence—a rape of the mind, a diversionary puzzle that absorbs all energy and emotion. This is passively violent control at its best.

Expertocracy not only controls thought and action by controlling language but also by attempting to reshape reality to fit its own guidelines.

One friend tells me about his experiences with a transactional therapist. "I come to him with these problems and he tells me, 'Oh, that's your child talking,' or, 'Now your parent is speaking,' or 'Yes, that's your adult now.' I think all that is very interesting, but when do I find out what to do about my problems?"

We've all had experiences like that with expertocrats. Our problems simply get redefined in and reduced to their current language, then fed back to us as though the translation would bring us some magical relief.

Expertocrats generate even more violence when they simply deny the reality we feel or twist it into a convenient brush-off. We still pay full fare for this trip. A friend of mine explained:

> I was going to this specialist for about six months, taking all the tests he could think of. He's a blood specialist, and I was having a hard time just staying awake and thought it had to be some kind of problem with my blood . . . anemia or something. The doctor did the tests and they cost a lot because he was a specialist. But I really had to find out what was the matter, because I just couldn't function.
>
> After about six months of coming to him and taking tests he began telling me that he had ninety-year-old patients with heart trouble who had more energy than me. He told me that it was patients like me that made doctors want to give up medicine. He said that I would be better off in psychotherapy and intimated that my problems were hypochondriac.
>
> But I managed to survive all that and demanded that he put me in a hospital and do every test there was to find out what was wrong with me. I was sure something was physically wrong. He continued to pressure and ridicule me, but finally gave in and put me in the hospital.
>
> In the hospital they found that I had serum hepatitis. They had to do a liver biopsy to find it, but they did and it explained why I had been so tired and lethargic.
>
> After the tests were concluded, my doctor comes in, and I

can't believe this, but he said, "You know, I had a hunch from the beginning that this might be the problem!"

The twilight zone of expertocratic blamelessness can drive a rational person to extremes of violence. Unfortunately, many people feel helpless to dent the expertocratic domain and turn their rage inward, on themselves.

Suicide in middle-class and more affluent families has become pandemic, especially among teenagers and young adults. So when a good friend's son killed himself with an overdose of pills, his death was not unique even though it came as a shock. Suburban and well-to-do young people have been dropping out of life like so many lemmings over the past decade. Some experts have analyzed and quantified the phenomenon while others tried to control the self-destruction.

What made this suicide so particularly tragic, aside from its devastating effect on my friend and his family, was that the young man had been a patient for the previous four years. During that time he had seen no fewer than eight separate doctors in an attempt to bring himself out of the panic and fear that dominated his life. With each move came a renewed promise, only to end up with the experts even more helpless to "break through" than the boy. After eight experts and eight "failures," the boy finally got the message and killed himself. He finally reached his limit. He had failed enough.

A week after the boy's death, his father got the last bill for services from the most recent psychiatrist, a bill for the Wednesday session of the previous week—the same Wednesday the boy killed himself.

Rationalizations and explanations are easy. The kid might have killed himself anyway. Maybe the therapy kept him alive all those years.

But maybe it didn't. Maybe it created the futility that led to his death. No one will ever know. What we do know is that four years of submission to the expertocracy ended badly and that the young son and the parents felt responsible. The experts remained totally blameless for having consumed so much time and money, only to see their efforts so clearly fail.

Again, as with so many "simple" tragedies, the violence is complex. The boy died from self-inflicted violence that had its roots somewhere between his own terrifying experiences and the expertocracy's inability to deal effectively with it. The family suffered the violence of the child's suicide and reacted in ways that his most recent analytic helper never probed. *They* were not his patients.

The family became both victims of the son's violence and carriers of violence out of the frustration and anger arising from the disappointment of their son and the failure of his hired helpers. The parents became volatile victims. Even though the boy's father never expressed this feeling, I know it dawned on him that maybe his son would be alive if he had not had expert help at all.

Intervention that ends as tragically as this cannot help but have elaborate consequences. But of all the possible recriminations and doubts, the experts felt the least of them and would be the last to consider or acknowledge the effects of their violence that became one young man's final statement to his world. That indifference is violent passivity, and it is disturbing. It is that kind of indifference that sends people to numerologists rather than psychologists. Or to the courts for some kind of redress for such flagrant irresponsibility.

The effectiveness of passive violence lies in the similarity between the violent act and some other necessary and legitimate action. It wears various covers well. In the case of the suicidal boy, there is a distinct difference between "professional distance" and personal indifference. Professional distance is psychologically necessary to the expert when lifesaving expertise involves pain and suffering. The psychiatrist must be detached to be effective. How could someone cut into another person, listen to people's psychic torment without crying, or at least grinding down a second molar, unless he detached himself emotionally? Personal indifference, on the other hand, is a way to rationalize ineffective actions and incompetence.

Experts are forgiven the necessary violence of their professions. The burdens of their jobs create understandable difficulties and limitations. Expertocrats use this absolution to excuse unnecessary and avoidable violence. People automatically forgive them, often to the point of apologizing to the expertocrat when they present him with problems more complicated than those he can comfortably handle. The expertocrat becomes the victim of the client's tragedy, a role reversal that carries with it inexpressible violence for the client.

A doctor who specializes in respiratory ailments and sees no relationship between his work and the fight for clean air is an expertocrat. His expertise becomes questionable and expertocratic when he refuses to use his status and power to deal with the economic or political issues that affect his patients. He doesn't see "superfluous" activity as his responsibility. He defines his work as narrowly as he can.

An "expert" in constitutional law becomes an expertocrat when he fails to protest a judge's gag-order action that denies reporters First Amendment protections. Any lawyer who continues to practice law under conditions that are illegal or that threaten constitutional protections is complying with the destruction of the law and has given up his right to be considered an advocate.

A 1975 Justice Department report stated that eighty percent of the reporters asked to comply with grand jury subpoenas complied willingly. The passive complicity of those journalists assured the future abuses they and others would suffer and destroyed their capacity to be effective in their roles as reporters. By complying with an order that took precedence over their professional responsibility they took their place in the expertocracy.

There is a very strong tendency for public officials to be bureaucrats and for authorities on particular subjects to be expertocrats. The exceptions are notable. A group of interns in Los Angeles withheld their services in hospitals until hospital conditions for the patients were upgraded. By this stand they jeopardized not only their internships but their futures as doctors. They went beyond their job descriptions and took an ethical position as to what they believed medicine must be. Their active assertion of principle morally validated their expertise. Having a superior knowledge of a subject, while maintaining or sustaining dangerous or destructive conditions, negates expertise. The essence of expertocracy is knowledge compromised by self-interest.

Lawyers have become the prototypes of expertocrats. Their self-interest prevents their being in the forefront of court or prison reform. They have become among the most "helpless" of all the professionals, and in the process people have lost respect for their claim to expertise. They are, along with most expertocrats, "survivors."

Once hired as an "advocate," the lawyer has become the victim of victims. More people than ever before are representing themselves in civil cases, according to one Ralph Nader task force report, because the time and money involved in hiring lawyers have made lawsuits for amounts under $10,000 "impractical." Many people who felt they had a legitimate claim against a business or individual were being forced to "settle" by lawyers, who were collecting fees even for this advice. Legal fees and lawyer-related delays have become major obstacles to civil justice.

Bar associations have become more active in advising people not to represent themselves, mounting full scale campaigns to frighten people out of "being your own lawyer." What they don't say is that legal malpractice suits charging "abandonment" (a term that refers to a lawyer's not showing up in court or otherwise dropping a case without notifying either the court or his client) have risen more than five hundred percent over the last few years.

No wonder that lawyers are rated near the bottom on every scale of public esteem, a phenomenon most likely translated into an even greater sense of victimization by legal practitioners.

AUTHOR'S NOTE

Many expertocrats aren't visible. To be fair I must say that the doctor, lawyer, and teacher are most easily seen and understood. They make it easier to communicate what is clearly a much more broadly based problem. Geologists, engineers, and architects, for instance, escape public scorn even when the hillside or oceanside homes they plan and design fall over cliffs or into the sea.

The expertocracy has us in a net. We depend on them, give them status, even look away from their lack of moral or ethical standards. We trust them with power while we exonerate them from responsibility. It's a paradoxical relationship reminiscent of mythological heroes, pharaohs, emperors, and kings. In a desperate desire to depend on the professionals among us, people have overlooked the reality, that the expertocracy represent only themselves. They are a self-interest group no better nor worse than any other.

"On the first day of the new school year, all the teachers in one private school received the following note from their principal:

Dear Teacher:
 I am a survivor of a concentration camp. My eyes saw what no man should witness.
 Gas chambers built by *learned* engineers.
 Children poisoned by *educated* physicians.
 Infants killed by *trained* nurses.
 Women and babies shot and burned by *high school* and *college* graduates.
 So, I am suspicious of education.
 My request is: Help your students become human. Your efforts must never produce learned monsters, skilled psychopaths, educated Eichmanns."

        Haim Ginot in *Teacher and Child*

There is both paradox and danger in opposing the expertocracy. The sheer numbers of expertocrats overwhelm democratic institutions, individual expression, and opposition to those institutions.

Andrei Sakharov, in his book *Alarm and Hope,* unwittingly explains America's loss of democratic consciousness by describing the Soviets' limits on dissent:

"Of course dissenters are few; how could it be otherwise in a state where everyone is either a hired hand of the government or a functionary, and all live in total dependence on the state? . . .

"Their [the dissenters'] activity is of interest to the whole world after decades of living next to the totalitarian colossus."

What future "colossus" may be in store for us may make itself clear if we fuse Sakharov's analysis of the self-interest of the Soviet totalitarian state that prevents dissent with a statistical trend in America.

In the early 1930s there was one government worker for every ten in industry. In the late 1940s the ratio was one to six. Since 1970 it has been one to four. According to some reports every other worker in America will be employed by some government agency by the mid-1980s.

Hannah Arendt emphasized the paradox of growing expertocratic control and historical American allegiance to individualism. Arendt argued that totalitarianism depends on a developed bureaucracy armed with modern technology. She could be describing our expertocracy.

In *The Origins of Totalitarianism,* she says that totalitarianism is designed to work on large masses of people who have been rendered rootless and controllable.

Most important, Arendt confirms the danger of idea-warped egalitarianism and its capacity to lead to authoritarian control. "Totalitarianism," she says, "attempts to reduce masses to a single controllable object." It is the victory of the expertocratic political axis over the private and individualistic "enemy."

When sociologist Robert Nisbet called for a restoration of traditional authority as the alternative to totalitarianism, he recognized that "the authority that is natural and basic to social organizations, neighborhoods, families, and voluntary organizations is being crowded out by government." He also saw that "there are more Americans who literally hate their government today than anything I have ever known of." Even considering public reaction to the New Deal, he said, "I have no recollection of people of all ages being either absolutely indifferent or outright hostile to government as they are today." He, too, predicted authoritarian rule if "traditional authority" wasn't re-established.

With every other American potentially a part of the expertocratically designed system, we would be controlled by a government in which we would participate in an authoritarian, totalitarian, experotcratic warp of democracy. "Of the people, by the people, and for the people" is likely to become "By the experts, through the bureaucrats, and over the people."

There is a dangerous reactionary force in this country that fears any intellectual effort or creation. It uses expertocratic failure and provocation to rage against genius and to degrade the intellectual.

Expertocrats are not intellectuals or geniuses but pretenders. They are to true genius what snake oil salesmen are to Drs. Fleming and Salk. (It may be that two definitions of "genius" are applicable here: the natural capacity for creative and original intellect and the existence of mutually opposed spirits, one good and one evil, that are supposed to attend a person throughout his life. While I'm using "true genius" to refer primarily to the first and more common definition, the other offers a somewhat metaphorical way to distinguish between the genius and the expertocrat—the good and the evil.) By linking the genius's potential for good to the expertocrat's talent for dispassionate destructiveness, the expertocracy has increased the likelihood of anti-intellectual backlash. After years of educational apprentice-ship in the art of strategic submissiveness, the intellectual is a ready scapegoat for the excesses of expertocratic violence.

Ivory tower intellectualism is not only a reality but a necessity. There must be people free to think and experiment and imagine without the constraints of business or government. But there is good reason to fear that the expertocracy will bring these towers down.

Anti-intellectual violence has followed almost every major revolutionary action or social upheaval, from America to China to Germany. It is not necessarily a considered cry for the blood of the creators but more likely a redirection of energy away from themselves by the same expertocrats who use creative genius to gain power. The pragmatism and self-centeredness of the expertocrat makes it axiomatic that he will choose a scapegoat to absorb the unfocused public rage he has created and fomented.

Academic and intellectual associations are violently passive and offer no help in making the necessary distinction between intellectual and expertocratic values. They refuse to assert their collective authority to disown incompetent and dangerous colleagues. Getting rid of the expertocrat without destroying the intellectual life of the country will be one of the most difficult tasks of this era. It will require more critical judgment from our citizens and an unwillingness to allow unaccountable, autocratic conglomerates to make decisions and allocate resources without the public's express permission.

Professional associations will have to enforce existing ethics. They will have to make everyone holding or aspiring to membership accountable to a clear moral code. While there has been some movement toward greater citizen participation in the decisions that have become the exclusive domain of the expertocracy, the movement overall has made little impact. Professional societies, as George Bernard Shaw said, are "conspiracies against the layman." Public participation in professional societies is essential to protect against corrupt self-interest.

Our educational system supports the expertocracy by favoring conformity and minimizing the importance of intellectual challenge, while advocating security, safety, and self-centeredness. It is, in short, the root and life support system of the self-serving expert. Intellectualism and genius are dangerous aberrations to the educational expertocracy. The fusion of the educational system to the federal, state, city, and privately contracted expertocracy has created an alliance that will be difficult to overcome. The prognosis is grim for training our young for critical analysis and non-expertocratic expertise.

People confuse their irrational fear of genuine scientific progress (genetics, biochemistry, and biophysics have always created Frankensteins at the same time that they offered answers to the nature of man and the universe) with the very rational fear of incompetent scientists, lawyers, politicians, and social theorists. That confusion has already led many of them to reject effective authority as well as inept and failing authority. This is the real danger: that our personal reactions to the experts' failure to advise us constructively about taxation, inflation, pollution, conservation, and crime will make us cynical about the work underway to cure cancer, control weather, and develop adequate and unpoisoned food and water supplies for the world's population. The violence that expertocratic bumbling and doubletalk creates in our daily lives is painful enough. But the violence to the planet that can come out of the reactionary destruction of our intellectual resources is incalculable.

In the doctor's office, I'm engaged in an anonymous conversation with the woman sitting next to me. She has just noticed the splashy cover of a magazine advertising an article about Richard Nixon's post-Watergate book. Our conversation gives way to a monologue about her resentment that Nixon "got off" and actually made money from the national disaster his administration left as a legacy.

"You know the worst part?" she asks, not waiting for my answer. "The worst part is that when they start cloning people, who do you think they'll make a million copies of? Nixon. That's who they'll clone. One million Nixons."

I asked her if she would feel the same way about cloning if scientists were about to clone thirteen Einsteins or six Albert Schweitzers or a dozen Madame Curies, but she wasn't listening. The disillusionment caused by one presidential band of expertocrats had invalidated the future of scientific exploration for her. If *he* was bad, they were all bad. That kind of generalized cynicism, created by expertocratic violence, opens the door wide to authoritarian and totalitarian control.

The rational and irrational had come together in this woman and the result was reactionary fear and anger. She is not alone. Given the obvious power of conscience-free expertocrats to turn scientific progress into unimagined nightmares, who's to say she's wrong?

In the same way that expertocrats have done violence to the people, people have used their cynicism and absurd expectations to do violence to their leaders. It may well have been the threat of this violence that caused many experts to seek refuge behind bureaucracies in the first place, by becoming expertocrats—truly a vicious circle.

Rah Rah Blacksheep

"The fate that awaits the creator,
after being ignored, neglected, despised,
is, luckily or unluckily according
to point of view, to be discovered
by the noncreative."
R. D. Laing, The Politics of Experience

"Show me a hero and I will write you a tragedy."
F. Scott Fitzgerald

We have emerged from the Age of Enlightenment, in which people began to feel that they could do something about their future by using their reason, to the Age of Anxiety, in which people feel there is little they can do about the countless circumstances that oppress them. One of the casualties of this evolution of thought is the hero. The hero is the victim of our time. The old bigger-than-life hero represented the ideal, an example of how mortal man could stretch himself beyond his everyday abilities. People saw themselves as capable, resourceful, or powerful and looked for heroes who could show the way. But as our society has become more complex and its functions more obscure, people understand less and less how it works. Unable to understand his own culture, the average person feels helpless to change anything significantly. Seeing his leaders in a similar quandary, he accepts (even values) helplessness and victimization. The idea of the hero has been sacrificed to our lowered expectations.

The new hero personifies victimization, the status quo, and retreat. He represents the way people *are,* no longer the possibilities of what they might *become.* The coinciding rise of narcissism and victimization has created the first mirror-victim-hero. The bigger-than-life hero first became an antagonistic anachronism and, finally, simply laughable.

The hero's present role, denying the individual's potential for changing society, began to evolve as more of the dangers of leadership and the futility of heroics became commonly known.

Gary Cooper's role in the movie *High Noon* reflected the dangers that classic heroes had to overcome. It foreshadowed the fate of many young activists who would soon take to the streets looking for justice and a successful battle with the bad guys, only to find some hard truths about Justice and The People.

Frank Miller is coming out of jail after many years, locked up there because of the Sheriff. The Sheriff is Gary Cooper, strong and moral. He has always done his duty as he's seen it and he's about to see it and do it again. Frank Miller has vowed to kill the Sheriff who sent him up. Our strong and moral hero, while showing some fear and trepidation, decides to stand his ground when the noon train comes in with Miller and his pent-up vengeance aboard.

The Sheriff's Quaker wife (Grace Kelly) is dutiful to a point, yet she has her limits. She tells Cooper that if he values his future with her, he will depart posthaste from this town before she ends up wearing widow's weeds. Cooper remains. The townsfolk are not only behind him, they're grateful for his help. Without him they don't stand a chance against Miller and his likes. They meet with him and praise his steadfastness, his courage, and his morality. They are behind him to a man. It's a warm and rousing unity. The bad guys must be dummies to come up against such collective determination.

But then Miller's advance guard, mean critters all of them, start arriving in town waiting for the noon train. The townspeople now have second thoughts. Maybe Miller's boys are coming into town just for a reunion and would leave the town alone if only Cooper wasn't there. Maybe it would be a good idea if Cooper left town. After all, they've got wives and children. They also value their lives, and none of them, it seems, believes much in the view from Boot Hill. So, after a few scenes of subtle cajoling, they tell Cooper to get the hell out of town. *He* is the troublemaker, expecting their support while bringing down a horrible fate on them for his own selfish reasons. If he wants to persist in carrying on a fight with the outlaw, he'll have to go it alone. They didn't think he was that hot a Sheriff anyway.

Who sticks with him? The town hooker, a kid, and a drunk. His wife is on her way out of town when the bad guy arrives but she does come through in the end. After Cooper is shot up, beat up, and just about blown away, his nonviolent wife, who has crept into hiding, shoots one of the killers in the back just seconds before he was about to do the same to hubby.

Cooper wins. The town comes out of the woodwork looking guilty and wanting to back the winner after he has won. The tin star is thrown into the dirt, and Cooper and Kelly go off into the sunset. Cooper has had an inkling of what Nietzsche realized some years before: "It's not from the strongest that harm comes to the strong, but from the weakest." The town is left to its own.

The theme of *High Noon* repeats itself throughout history, mythology, and popular literature. The savior comes from the people, is revered by the people, leads the people, is killed or weakened by the people, and, once out of their midst, is revered again. Over and over, when there is a problem, there is a person of vision, a good guy who can solve the problem. There are the people in whose name the good guy confronts the problem, and it's these same people who inevitably abandon the good guy or plot to get rid of him in the name of purity, justice, or peace. While solving the problem, the good guy becomes the bad guy in the eyes of the people. The most recent good guy, however, if he survives his lonely perils (or survives the aid of hookers, kids, or nonviolent wives), doesn't think the results were really worth his trouble.

Going back four thousand years to the Babylonian myth, *Enuma Elish,* we see the gods hire a young novice to kill a threatening evil force. They find him so dangerous that when he succeeds they "reward" him by giving him the burdens of all their fifty gods (another way of running him out of town). In Old English literature, when Beowulf defeats the beast Grendel (another pressing evil), he is said to deserve kingship because no one knows what else to do with so capable a person outside of combat. Whether through kingship or deportation, the hero is removed from the ranks of the people, kicked upstairs or out of town.

The Japanese Samurai legends often end with the savior-warrior more feared and detested than the evil he defeated. And, of course, we can't forget the crucifixion of Jesus Christ.

The message is universal. The candidates for good guy get the same message that Bugs Bunny keeps giving to Elmer Fudd. If you walk out on a limb, someone will saw it off.

A common concern of both the civil rights and the student movements of the sixties was that of heroes. The civil rights movement was looking for righteous, ignored heroes who had been left out of the history books. The student movement was looking very critically at the people who appeared in the history books as heroes but whose everyday character traits had been carefully overlooked. One group was looking for the people among them who were heroes and the other was looking at the heroes who could be leveled into people.

Both groups came out of the sixties with a common experience and self-assessment. In a return to pre-enlightenment thought, they rediscovered the idea that one person can do nothing to make major changes in the world. Many of these young people had never known prolonged frustration or futility before, coming as they did from the second generation of the educated and the privileged. Once they felt the overwhelming helplessness in their romantic confrontation with the reality of a complex and violent society, they became committed non-believers in heroics. No one, not even a fantasy hero, could do what they couldn't do.

There are few things as powerful and disabling to the convert as the cynicism that replaces altruism. Most of the activists, poorly educated in the complexities of their government, came to the cynical conclusion that visible leadership was only a moving target, while invisible and elusive leadership made all the important decisions. For some who decided they'd rather quit than continue to fight, this realization pushed them into the religious and psychological cults of the seventies. If they were going to be controlled anyway, many decided, they might as well get some sense of belonging and security in exchange for individual submission.

Armies used to fight "for the right" on behalf of God or country, against obvious bad guys with bad ideas. In fact, the lawyers, detectives, police, doctors, and other good guys we watch on television, see in the movies, or read about are in similar situations to the ones armies used to face. They are faced with one problem. Its solution may be elusive but the problem is clear. Once the problem or the mystery is solved, the job is done. These stories are not presented as myths but they create a myth. We expect our social and national problems to be as simple. If only we could find *the key, the answer,* or *the leader,* our problems can be solved. But there is no one key or one answer and we haven't reckoned with that reality yet. Legions of insoluble problems now attack the individual, who finds it hard to justify blaming any one of them for his plight (even if he could pick one out of the many). For one person or even a group of people to fight invisible armies is futile. Personal heroics are foolish. The majestic hero is now played by King Kong, a giant too fantastic to threaten anyone's passivity.

World and national leaders and heroes seem self-deceptive to a protected generation whose activism arose from a most unrealistic view of mankind and social change. They became converts to a grim realism. *They* were the heroes and they were failing, even though they were "the best and the brightest." If they couldn't do the job, no one could. Anyone attempting to attack as big a problem as poverty or war, after they had failed in their attempts, became a crazy egotist.

Heroes became impossible to identify, since it was difficult to say what was good or bad. There were no absolute values and no absolute heroes. Every person and incident was "graded on the curve" (the average getting the biggest share), and the hero was no exception. Now there were "average" heroes—once a contradiction in terms. The hero became everyone and no one. It became unacceptable for a hero to make it on his own. The hero, as we knew him, ceased to exist. The new hero became a vulnerable figure no better than the rest of us. Saul Bellow's *Herzog,* a failure as a husband, father, lover, and teacher, is redeemed by his persistence. He is a hero simply because he *survives.*

I asked an avid sports fan and friend of mine about the changes in sports heroes over the past twenty years. It seemed to me that the idolizing of players like Joe DiMaggio, Mickey Mantle, Babe

Ruth, Lou Gehrig, and Willie Mays had not carried over to Reggie Jackson, Pete Rose, and Steve Garvey, the new superstars. I wanted to know why. What had happened to the heroes people used to find in sports?

"They started making too much money," my friend said without giving it a second thought. "They used to make a lot of money, but not the way they do now.

"And they also used to be bound to their teams. Now they're 'free.' They can negotiate for better money with another team. They don't have the hometown loyalty that the old stars used to have, mostly because the rules have changed and they have no allegiance to fans or ballparks."

"But don't more and more people watch them on TV?" I asked.

"Yeah, TV and radio have more sports events than ever before. People haven't stopped watching sports. If anything, they're watching more sports than ever. It's just the players who have lost their impact. You've still got good players. Maybe as good as or better than the ones who used to be everyone's heroes. But they're on their own, they're very rich, and they're free. There's not much that people can identify with anymore."

Will Rogers said, "We can't all be heroes, because somebody has to sit on the curb and clap as they go by." People have begun to sit on the curb and clap for themselves. To be a hero no longer means a reach but a reflection. Anyone can play.

If it is a fundamental process of leadership to "make conscious what lies unconscious," as James MacGregor Burns suggests in his book *Leadership,* the future hero-leader may well be a combination of Woody Allen and Charles Manson—a charming, victimized psychopath. The Woody Allen image is already captivating the educated and affluent with his personification of helplessness, vulnerability, and futility. The terrorist-hero is not far behind and will reflect the pent-up violence of the Flock. The victim-hero is an interim figure, filling in between the idealized moral hero and the nihilist hero to come.

Looking at the present trends I see a possibility that the terrorist-hero will be the hero of this decade. It would serve us well to understand how close this publicly abhorred figure is to becoming an extension of the victim-hero. There are many reports of terrorist hostages who end up identifying with and even rooting for their captors. They have become convinced that their captors are even more victimized than themselves. (Police are seeing this same phenomena in kidnapping victims.)

The terrorist lives just over the line from the victim, who when pushed to the extreme can resort to violence, justified in self-defense. When amorphous oppression hits the privileged middle-class victim, the result is the raw material for terrorism.

Terrorism is undoubtedly one of the most socially significant and dangerous results of the link between cold war tactics and the alienated bourgeoisie. Since the hero reflects the aspirations of the worshiper, and since victimization allows and even excuses violent action to people who otherwise think of themselves as non-violent, the terrorist-hero, offering a vicarious release of generalized, accumulated violence, seems imminent. The "advantage" of the terrorist-hero over the violent moralist-hero lies in the terrorist's absence of moral or ethical demands on the people for whom he serves as surrogate. The terrorist-hero is a reactionary and represents violence always in self-defense, uncluttered by any obligations to plans or principles. Because of this, the terrorist-hero is instantly disposable and replaceable. He is, in effect, biodegradable.

Many lower-class and blue-collar workers still seek out classical moral heroes and the glorification of personal power seen in the film characters of Clint Eastwood, Charles Bronson, and others who, despite the violence of their films, appeal essentially to optimism. The individual can overcome corruption, greed, and the violence of the expertocracy, can overcome all the existing social odds, and win. The trucker and the "outlaw" country-western singer are "real life" examples of these fictional characters. The more education people have, the less likely they are to see the individual as a possible winner. The working class somehow still believes in individual potential for social change which the middle class has abandoned.

Upper-middle-class Americans tend to be rootless and isolated from one another, at the same time representing strong "other-directed" values. As David Reisman observes in *The Ethics of*

Collectivism, "The burden of being one's own arbiter of taste has been removed." It's ironic that the avant-garde of the egocentric society is anti-individualist. Maybe the answer to this lies in an idea warp created by the "human potential movement." It emphasizes obsession with the self and concentrates on inner states as if they were innately valuable. It ignores the limits that this egotism sets on dealing with others. It plays down initiative and leadership in favor of "laying back," "hanging loose," and "letting go."

Personal change does not bring automatic changes in the world outside. Realizing this, when one is cornered in the recesses of the self, can lead to explosive outrage and "revenge." The individual becomes a terrorist for his own cause. He has been victimized by the ideology of self-knowledge and inner peace. The human potential movement has created a nightmare of lonely, selfish people quarreling for power. By refusing to deal directly with social issues or the realities of coexistence, the movement creates, instead, a confused and violence-prone victim.

Konrad Lorenz, the Nobel Prize-winning animal behaviorist, is convinced that crime and terrorism are surging because people are unable to establish close friendships. According to Lorenz, this affects the kinds of heroes and leaders people need and attract (an opinion that supports the possibility of future "terrorist-heroes").

"The capability of creating personal ties is atrophying," Dr. Lorenz said in an interview. "Restraints on aggressivity depend on personal acquaintance." Contrary to the beliefs of members of the human potential movement, "personal acquaintance" does not mean acquaintance with oneself alone while social trends, morality, and ethics are given up to group consensus.

To one part of our society, rooted in "traditional" American values, the individual hero is still a possibility. It is willing to accept a hero who may intrude on other people to assert leadership and accept the consequences.

To another part, larger, perhaps, the hero merely represents their vested interest in helplessness and futility.

*   *   *

The common elements of the hero/leader tales help explain why leadership and heroes are in such short supply. The people, it often turns out, want their dirty work done for them or power brought to them—delivered like the morning paper in suburbia. This collection of violent passivity has just one condition for anyone unwise enough to assume the role of hero/leader. The condition under which the People will be led is this: Don't endanger or disrupt us while you are making changes for us. If the hero meets this condition, the People may collaborate with him.

As soon as people are forced to participate in resolving their own predicament, as soon as they realize that they have to *do* something (go to meetings, boycott, strike, work), they demand to be convinced 1) that their enemy is really bad, 2) that their enemy is really worth fighting, and 3) that their hero-leader is sincere, honest, and pure. They begin to evaluate the problem in face of the *real* stakes.

Should they stick with the farmworkers boycott? Should they stick with the clean air committee? Should they stick with Jesus Christ?

"Is it really worth it after all?"

"We've got enough responsibilities of our own."

"Who is this guy, anyway, and why is he bugging us?"

Greener Pastures:
Relearning Relationships

"No creature who began as a mathematical improbability,
who was selected through millions of years of unprecedented
environmental hardship and change for ruggedness, ruthlessness,
cunning and adaptability, and who in the short ten
thousand years of what we may still call civilization has achieved
such wonders as we find about us, may be regarded as a
creature without promise."

Robert Ardrey, African Genesis

Before interpersonal warfare ends in some apocalyptic armistice, we're going to have to deal with the trail of broken promises that have made us complex victims. Nonviolent relationships can exist only when the people involved have a sense of their own competence, an ability to depend on other people, and a capacity to be depended upon. As things stand, the likelihood of a speedy peace seems pretty remote. But if we've learned anything as a species it is to expect the unexpected. One of the less gruesome resolutions of the pandemic violence would be that we'd come to understand it, know what needs it meets, and find some more productive way of dealing with it than the ones we have created in our existing social institutions.

Most of us have been through at least as many disappointments as we have institutions. There is something about the systems that we create and support that keeps us supporting them, however grudgingly, even as we are ignored, abused, or neglected by them. While many people have learned to accept the self-perpetuating system, we haven't detached ourselves from the violence this realization feeds. We have become subservient to institutions that have failed. Too often we are the injured victims of our own spoiled dreams.

Margaret Mead once said, "We need to recognize that most of the reform measures initiated during the early part of the century have gone sour. We need to know why. I suggest this was because we tried to protect (people) from a bad system instead of trying to alter the whole system."

She observed that despite well-intentioned reforms, new abuses developed. That seems to be a pattern. Knowing of this pattern braces us for disappointment while we yearn for reliability. We want to depend on the institutions that take so much from us, be we know we can't. We know that organizations become separate, self-centered organisms, growing as large as they can, consuming as much as we will let them, and offering as little as possible in return. What we created and sustained to depend on has become, instead, a burden, offering a fragile illusion of dependability.

Somehow we must stop endowing institutions with hopes and powers that are bound to fail. Practical goals can only be fulfilled when we cease to be victims, find power within ourselves, and stop seeing power as universally oppressive. In assuming more power we will demand more accountability and less willingly accept the subtle violence in too many personal relationships. Institutions can then be limited to the functions we need them to perform: teaching, health care, law enforcement, and spiritual encouragement.

By finding fewer excuses for our own failure, we will become less tolerant of our institutions' failures, creating a sharp system of checks and balances that does not exist now. By setting standards for ourselves we will also demand them of our institutions.

Realistically, we cannot expect institutions to welcome us as occasional dependents when we know there are few, if any, persons within them who are willing to assume more responsibility than we are. The institution, after all, only reflects the people who make and support it. Weak and self-centered people created and perpetuate inept and self-serving institutions. We not only don't get what we pay for but we don't get what we need. The foolish institutional fantasy has helped produce inadequate and untrusting people and causes the violence that comes from frustration.

One way we may be able to see the contrast between the ideal and the real relationship between people and their institutions is to look at the purest, most simplified example: the cult. While many are caricatures of group dependency and are destructive to their members and the surrounding society, many others show what group dependency can offer spiritually and materially. Cults have proliferated over the last twenty years as people have become disillusioned with organized religion and social organizations. People began to drop out of established movements and religions and became disciples of new prophets and visionaries. These leaders expressed not only the disillusionment of their followers but also their burning need to be a part of something bigger than their alienated selves. They offered "meaning" in a world becoming incomprehensibly complex and absurd. If existing institutions had not alienated people so totally, they could have helped to express and examine the growing complexities, and people would have been better educated and less fearful of rapid change. But the institutions, many of them once labeled "cults" themselves, had ossified, lost touch with their original constituencies, and had become islands of self-justifying failure and corruption.

The political scandals, undeclared wars, and system breakdowns that have become the everyday experience of generations of Americans didn't *create* disaffection but *focused* the disaffection that had existed for years. The Nixon excesses weren't unique instances of corruption that led to instant social reaction. They were themselves reactions to less obvious excesses that our institutions had covered and rationalized over many years. Only when these excesses could no longer be denied did established institutions acknowledge them. But they had already lost the majority of Americans to self-involvement or to the collective security of new cults. The "me generation" was a creation of despair. There was no place left to go but inward. For many people, unwilling or unable to sustain themselves as sheep outside the flock, the cult was a place to come in from the cold.

The cult has become the institutional pimp to prostituted selves. It takes care of its followers, loves them, gives them a job to do, and may even gratify their low self-esteem by physically or psychologically abusing them. All the members have to do is give up their bodies, their worldly possessions, and their identity. For many people already disintegrated by social institutions that have failed them, identity is nothing much to lose. The cult and the pimp offer survival and purpose.

Sometimes the cult becomes violent, first in subtle ways, bullying and berating deviant members, then in more aggressive terrorist tactics. The true believers' surprise at the ferocity of the once peaceful and idealistic cult is reflected in defections from one cult to another. This often happens when the cult leader, unsure of his dependent following, unmasks himself and exposes the totalitarian brute, strengthened by outside "enemies" into "the Protector."

The people we have to worry about are the ones who have given into the brute, have spent their resistance, or had none to begin with. These are the fanatics. They are the products of institutions, people who exist only for the good of whomever they serve. They do not exist in any way but to perpetuate the cult-pimp. They become the cult. They live and die for it. They have no will but the will of the Protector, and the Protector has the power to destroy them.

The cult is an important model because it shows us in miniature the process of individual submission to the collective and the extremes to which this submission may lead. It also magnifies our own relationships with institutions and our motives for accepting unacceptable conditions. For many of us it's the only game in town. Relearning relationships means rethinking our personal and institutional ties and giving a careful look to whether there might really be something else.

It's important to understand some of the psychological roots of violence that are later complicated by our social involvements. One of the greatest conflicts, producing much violence, is that between the virtue of self-assertion and our need for dependency. Although our "national character" emphasizes the virtues of individuality, we are conditioned to conform and be dependent. As if things were not confusing enough, we're not allowed to fulfill either of these stated values. Children may neither exist on their own nor depend for long or with any reliability on anyone else. What we call extended childhood is really a state of extended anxiety in which young people are kept in an undefined panic looking for ways to understand and control an overwhelming and hostile environment. They become like the shark, moving endlessly through the waters without sleep, searching for whatever can be consumed to stay alive.

The helpless human infant cannot develop self-reliance before it is able to rely on others. Unlike many other "lower" animals, the human infant can't feed itself, see to its own needs for warmth or shelter, or otherwise protect itself from danger. The dependency is complete. The "inferiority" we're born with is quite real. Its continuation, however, into childhood, adolescence, and adulthood is a cultural warp.

Since parents also wish to be dependent their children feel enormous shame for receiving or even wanting such protection and support. This eventually leads them to feel victimized, making them search for even greater dependency. Poet Lawrence Ferlinghetti in his poem "Lost Parents" describes the fate of "throw-away" children:

> . . . who
>
> left to their own devices
> in a beach house at Malibu
> grew up and dropped out into Nothing
> in a Jungian search
> for lost parents
>
> their own age

As they search they get older, and it becomes less and less reasonable to seek dependency. Thus they become increasingly guilty, passive, and enraged. The evolution of a successful and complete personality, able to be both dependent and dependable, is interrupted.

We want to be seen, heard, and felt, and we have a strong desire to be known and understood as individuals. Yet we also want to be cared for, nurtured, and supported. When both of these needs are frustrated, as they often are, the result is an incompetent, uncaring self. It is the mainspring of violence.

In my search for the connections between passivity and violence I discovered that a major concept of human feeling easily expressed in everyday Japanese has totally resisted translation into a Western language (or thought). The Japanese psychiatrist Dr. Takeo Doi has explored and defined an area of the psyche which has previously received little attention. His work, written when he was a visiting scientist in the National Institute of Mental Health and a fellow at the Menninger Foundation, suggests what may be a missing link in American social and psychological development and a major root of violence.

Dr. Doi's work, *The Structure of Amae,* is focused on an emotion central to the Japanese experience. *Amae* refers to the indulging, passive love that surrounds and supports the individual in a group, whether family, neighborhood, or the world at large.

To be *amaeru,* to assume the right to presume upon a relationship, openly and without shame, is to fulfill a basic human need. The passively violent tactics of the Flock are distortions of *amaeru,* covert manipulations of dependency. The ability of people to find *amae* in some social institution, be it within a friendship, a family or some other constructive constellation of people, seems essential in reversing the growing trend toward violence. In Dr. Doi's terms, if a child cannot be *amaeru,* if it cannot presume upon dependency, it will not be able to offer *amae* to others.

There is a deeply rooted connection between the frustrated right to presume upon a relationship and the violence that often erupts in an effort to enforce that right covertly. What we can't even admit to wanting becomes so strong a need that we must seize it strategically. Denial of a basic need usually produces a distorted response later.

We are taught that our basic needs include food, water, and sleep. We are also taught that we're social animals and that "social" means having some vague affinity for cooperation. But the need to belong, with all its presumption of and demands for reciprocity, is not emphasized in our culture.

Once we are no longer children, expressing a need to be *amaeru* in American society is an admission of weakness, a violation of the pioneer image of self-reliance. Even though many of us feel that weakness and create and perpetuate relationships that reinforce that feeling, the craving for a relationship that could nurture us and give us strength is still the most tortuous longing in our lives.

The Flock is a collection of people who feel powerless and disaffected. It is a distortion, a warp of the interconnected group, of the open and shameless human need to presume on relationships. It offers the antithesis of *amaeru* and perpetuates precisely the destructive conditions that caused it to exist. It attempts to create by passive force what cultural precedent has denied.

While Dr. Doi's work bridged my own experiences with passive violence and my need to find interdependence, there are other important affirmations of the connection between violence and belonging. Arthur Koestler, considering man's dual nature in his book *Janus,* sheds light on the "self-assertive" and "integrative" tendencies that keep us in equilibrium. Each of these tendencies, according to Koestler, has its own rules and predispositions. They help to define us as unique individuals while also connecting us with social groups.

Koestler's argument in support of this duality is overwhelming. He progresses down the scale of life forms and forces and finds duplications of the same ordered duality he sees in the human "holon" (a functional unit that is more than the sum of its parts and at the same time part of some larger whole). Each cell in the body is a semi-autonomous unit possessing its own "self-assertive" DNA. Still, each cell is part of a larger unit, and its survival is directly connected to the well-being of its environment.

This duality, when observed through the Japanese concept of *amae,* offers us a unique view of the dynamics of passive violence, which can be seen as a distortion of self-assertion and a frustration of interconnection. Clearly we need to find a way to assert ourselves within an *accepting* and *depending* group.

In the web of human relationships the competent self doesn't exist apart from an ability to depend on others. But psychologists who search for human potential stop short of mutual dependency in their "exercises." The classic "exercise" for trust and dependency is for one person to fall back and be caught by another person or a group. This falling back is at first resisted and then gets to feel good. The "faller" spends a lot of time describing the sensation of being caught, of developing "positive dependency." What isn't generally considered in this exercise is at least as important: the feelings of the person doing the catching.

In J. D. Salinger's *The Catcher in the Rye,* Holden Caulfield captures the joy of being "the catcher" in a fantasy he defensively shares with us:

> "I keep picturing all these little kids playing some game in this big field of rye and all. Thousands of little kids, and nobody's around—nobody big, I mean—except me. And I'm standing on the edge of some crazy cliff. What I have to do, I have to catch everybody as they start to go over the cliff—I mean if they're running and they don't look where they're going I have to come out from somewhere and *catch* them. That's all I'd do all day. I'd just be the catcher in the rye and all. I know it's crazy, but that's the only thing I'd really like to be. I know it's crazy. . . ."

But it's not crazy. There are good feelings that come from being *dependable,* even though this aspect of the human relationship is rarely discovered in any positive way and seems to have few rewards in our culture. Psychotherapists spend a lot of time on the patients' feelings of dependency. But little time, if any, is spent on the feelings the therapist gets from being depended upon. This is an important model but is strangely avoided by most therapists. To reach these feelings and to incorporate them into our everyday experience we may have to develop our own exercise. One safe and easy place to start is to look at a pet and search for the good feelings that come from that pet's dependence: sitting on your lap or waiting for food that you prepare and give them.

There's a cat I've come to know who makes his dependency so clear I love to be there for him. Yet he is also independent. He jumps on my lap, openly using me as his host, and as he lies there purring he squints straight into the face of his "pillow." Face to face, he maintains his own very clear self. It's a pleasure to be so constructively and openly used by him.

The satisfaction that comes with feeding and caring for an

animal can, of course, be transferred to a human, particularly a small one, someone young enough to accept dependency as part of the human condition. As people get older they get more resistant to being dependent, even though they may have a more critical need for dependency.

I was leading a therapy group of teenagers and young adults. In the group were three student therapists.

One of the teenagers was in a crisis. George was a leader of his high school class and well liked. His school work had improved significantly over the past year. He was in the group because he was having some serious problems at home and had been on the verge of moving out on his own when everything started going wrong. He failed to keep up his social relationships and leadership obligations, his classwork stopped completely, and he gave up his plans to move out of his parents' home.

After some resistance, he finally came out with the problem. He was almost eighteen years old, and that meant he wasn't a kid anymore. He would be legally responsible in the eyes of the law. And the prospect of being a certified adult terrified him. He was in a total and uncontrollable panic.

Everything about being an adult was bad. It was all responsibility and no fun. It was all liability and no benefits. People just expected more and more, "until I feel like I'm going to be locked up in jail," he explained. He saw nothing good about his future, only people demanding and expecting things from him—things, not coincidentally, he had never been able to expect from his family.

The student therapists chimed in with comments on "the brighter side" of being adult. They weren't convincing. Except for some feeble attempts at describing the "greater options" in adulthood, the adults eventually and unwittingly confirmed all George's worst fears. The time when it was all right to depend on someone (even if it didn't work out) was giving way to a life sentence of being depended on, and George wasn't ready for such stiff punishment.

George's crisis is repeated in thousands of therapists' offices every day. But most of the people in crisis are two or three times

George's age, all looking for something or some place that will let them be children again. In traditional Japan they wouldn't have to identify dependency with childhood alone and wouldn't be in such conflict about "regressing." They wouldn't carry around feelings of guilt or disorientation about wanting to be dependent, whatever their age.

Never finding this in our culture, adult responsibility becomes an empty and terrifying burden.

Disillusionment in the search for dependency comes when people looking for *amaeru* don't find a person or group that can give and take dependence. A sad nomadic search leads people from group to group, or, even sadder, into seclusion.

We need to create new ways for people to *live* in mutual dependence, and for leadership and individuality to thrive. People can "rehabilitate" themselves, in the best sense of that word, can change from free-floating and violent loners to part of a supporting system that can accept as well as make demands.

In most groups leaders become burdened with dependency and begin to deny and reject it, saying finally that they are only "guides," "facilitators," and other temporary posts on which people can lean. Group leaders are leveled by the demands put on them. When they talk to each other they often speak of "burning out" or feeling consumed by their flock.

I don't believe that any cooperative effort, planned community, workplace, political group, or government office can flourish unless its participants feel not only comfortable but delighted with being dependable or *amaeru*. Without that ingredient all participants will simply be used up by the experience instead of being renewed by it. They will exhaust their leaders and seek something else that seems to offer a more "successful" dependence.

In the meantime the inequity of one-way dependency consumes the one—or those few—who found initial pleasure or reward in giving. Having no sense of reciprocity, they can't transmit the pleasure at being dependable to the group, any more than the majority can communicate the pleasure of dependence. The group, having no positive frame of reference, degenerates.

Dependability is rejected as being "hassled" or on a "power trip," and the group perpetuates its own feelings of futility.

The antidote to that futility and the violence that often stems from it lies in developing a capacity for mutual dependability. For if isolation and nihilism can create violence born of anxiety, victimization, and fear, then competence and a sense of community are likely ways to achieve a happier survival.

If we were able to develop strong feelings of dependability we would get such a positive reaction that we could dramatically change our vulnerability to and involvement in passive violence. Our sphere of influence would increase as we felt more *able* (and less shrunk). We would demand more accountability from our experts, because we would be demanding more from ourselves. (Remember that weak people produce and support weak institutions.) The surer we were of our capabilities, the less we would be leveled. And the more we resisted being put down and leveling others, the better we could understand both the problems and pleasures of leadership.

Developing *capabilities* doesn't mean taking on impossible burdens. Unrealistic expectations of oneself can only increase futility and frustration and are self-defeating. I'm suggesting that we assume the *smallest possible commitment* to the "integrative" self. If that works out, a person can increase his acceptance of dependability and expand his positive nurturing potential.

I offer this suggestion out of my own experience, not as a panacea to ward off the evils of violence. It is not the answer to violence, passive or active. (Looking for *the* answer to any social or psychological problem *is* a social and psychological problem.) But I know that as soon as I was in a position to support young people with all their different needs and personalities, I was better able to see and control much of my own "unseen" oppression. There is something liberating about giving into the integrative impulse which isn't found in self-assertion alone.

We don't solve all our problems by feeling competent and dependable, but somehow we are better able to cope. We no longer see ourselves as victims, and this may be most important of all in helping us resist passively violent tactics.

The Flock and the Violent Sheep may always be with us. The

fight for survival may intensify and the invisible barbs and unseen gauntlets will not disappear. But people, connected to even the smallest network of supportive dependency and aware of the forces that exist to pull them apart, can respond better. They will be less willing victims, unsatisfied with life in the flock.

While we've been planning for our futures and studying our past, our national character has changed, like the caterpillar in the cocoon. Passive violence is one way of keeping our equilibrium while changing.

There is a homily: "Life is what's happening while you're making other plans." While we have been making other plans, we have become passively violent without knowing it. Now that we have some idea of our present condition, we can choose to do something about it. Or we can go on, under cover, pretending that the violence we are part of doesn't exist.

Our metamorphosis from boastful cowboy to cowering bureaucrat may be complete. Then again, there may be a more beautiful specimen to emerge from the cocoon somewhere in the future. Either way, the responsibility for what we become is ours.